PRESENTED TO:

Hannah Mullet (Claire)

FROM:

Believability Award

DATE:

Saturday, May 3, 2025

"The story of *Little Women* has always been the literary form of a cozy blanket from which generations of readers can seek comfort and warmth time and again. In this new devotional, Rachel brilliantly draws parallels between the scriptures and the most memorable excerpts of the beloved yet bittersweet classic. And just like the original story, this new book has the power to captivate hearts for years to come."

–Jen Smith, book collector, photographer, and curator of Storybook Style (@storybookstyle)

"Rachel Dodge has a way of making you feel as though you're with an old friend, chatting about life and love and faith over a cup of tea. *The Little Woman Devotional* is no exception. The moment you open its pages, you're swept into a well-loved favorite and with that comes all the comfortable, warm feelings of Christmas dinner and fireside conversations. This isn't merely a charming tribute to the Marches, though. Rachel has woven eternal truths into each passage in an encouraging and gentle bid to help you see past the story. To think more deeply about what you initially read. It's the perfect book for any young lady in your life but I challenge you to not fall in love with it yourself."

–Kimberly Duffy, author of *A Tapestry of Light* and *Every Word Unsaid*

"This is a charming devotional that brought back fond memories of my first reading of *Little Women* as a girl. I especially appreciated the prayers and personal applications at the end of each section. The book will become a treasured addition to your devotional library. Buy a copy for someone you love. Within its pages, faith, hope, and love abound."

–Shirley Raye Redmond, author of *Courageous World Changers: 50 True Stories of Daring Women of God,* the 2021 children's book recipient of the *Christianity Today* Book Award

"Rachel Dodge has given us a great gift in *The Little Women Devotional*. Reading these pages is like having a cozy chat with a friend by the fire. Dodge connects Alcott's classic about the March girls' life with our own spiritual lives in a beautiful, grace-filled, and encouraging way. I plan to buy a copy for every dear sister and friend I know!"

–Carrie Stephens, author of *Holy Guacamole*

"When I heard that Rachel Dodge was writing a devotional based on *Little Women*, I couldn't wait to read it. The book was even more wonderful than I expected. Rachel has a special gift for drawing biblical truths out of classic stories in a way that makes readers appreciate them in a deeper way. *The Little Women Devotional* invites those who have already fallen in love with Meg, Jo, Beth, Amy, Marmie, and Laurie to see how their adventures, lessons, and losses reflect God's grace and work in all of our lives. This is a perfect book for women to read with their daughters, sisters, friends, or alone while drawing closer to Jesus."

–Jeanette Hanscome, author of *Suddenly Single Mom: 52 Messages of Hope, Grace, and Promise*

"This beautiful devotional is Truth-filled and God-honoring. It highlights events and conversations in the chapters and also goes in depth into scripture themes throughout the book. I have purchased the author's *Anne of Green Gables* and Jane Austen devotionals as well. They are simply wonderful and I really can't recommend them enough!"

–Lucy McCracken, artist, designer, and literary gift shop owner
at Lucy in the Sky Creations (@lucyintheskycreations)

"My own daughter who has read the novel *Little Women* numerous times was struck by how each chapter in the March sisters' lives apply to so much in her life. Her first comments to me were how delighted she was to find so many lessons in this devotional that applied to her no matter how different her situations are than the characters in the book. This devotional encourages girls to think deeply not only about their reading but about their lives and relationships with God."

–Lea Ann Garfias, author of *Everything You
Need to Know About Homeschooling*

"As a Homeschool Mom and road school travel blogger, I classify *The Little Woman Devotional* as an heirloom treasure. I found myself curled up in a blanket with my kids and coffee in the morning, being transported back in time. Each devotion provoked amazing conversation and teaching moments. This devotional and Rachel Dodge's other classic devotionals will be a staple in our family's library. I highly recommend them to be in yours."

–Bethannah Guzman, blogger and designer at BethannahGuzman.com
and @lovebethannah on Instagram

"Rachel Dodge has a gift for connecting the greatest classic book of all time–the Bible–with the characters and themes of the beloved classics. In this luminous devotional, each day she links a story or anecdote from *Little Women* and ties it into scripture, making both the novel and the Bible come alive in a new way. The best part for me is the daily personal applications, which allow me to live out new truths gleaned from the pages of God's Word and one of my all-time most cherished novels. It was a joy to meet again with Marmee, Meg, Jo, Beth and Amy (not to mention Laurie and Professor Bhaer) as I drew closer to God's loving, guiding heart."

—Lorilee Craker, the author of 15 books, including *Anne of Green Gables,
My Daughter and Me: What My Favorite Book Taught Me
About Grace, Belonging and the Orphan in Us All*

THE
Little
Women
DEVOTIONAL

A CHAPTER-BY-CHAPTER COMPANION TO
Louisa May Alcott's
BELOVED CLASSIC

RACHEL DODGE

BARBOUR
PUBLISHING

Print ISBN 978-1-63609-096-2

Cover and interior illustrations: Miriam Serafin, Advocate Art, Inc.

Published by Barbour Publishing, Inc., 1810 Barbour Drive, Uhrichsville, Ohio 44683, www.barbourbooks.com

Our mission is to inspire the world with the life-changing message of the Bible.

Printed in China.

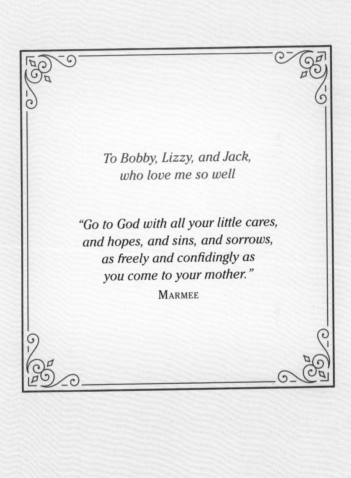

To Bobby, Lizzy, and Jack,
who love me so well

"Go to God with all your little cares,
and hopes, and sins, and sorrows,
as freely and confidingly as
you come to your mother."
MARMEE

Contents

A *Little Women* Welcome 11

Day 1: Begin Again in Earnest 14

Day 2: The Least of These 18

Day 3: Burnt Curls and Ballroom Twirls 23

Day 4: A Cure for the Grumps 27

Day 5: Meet the Neighbors 31

Day 6: Making Music with Our Lives 35

Day 7: Pickled Limes and Bitter Times 40

Day 8: The Sincerest Prayer 44

Day 9: All Dolled Up 49

Day 10: Make Room for More 53

Day 11: Lounging and Larking 58

Day 12: Pin It to Your Heart 62

Day 13: Living Examples 66

Day 14: Fledgling Dreams 70

Day 15: Christ in the Crisis 74

Day 16: Never Fatherless 79

Day 17: Old Habits 83

Day 18: A Lifeline 88

Day 19: Sacred Spaces 92

Day 20: Seasons of Change 96

Day 21: New Leaves 100

Day 22: One Drop More 104

Day 23: Love Worth Fighting For 109

Day 24: Wonderful Counselors 113

Day 25: Adorned with Love 117

Day 26: Fruitful Failures 122

Day 27: Groceries and Gowns 126

Day 28: Jelly Stains and Growing Pains 130

Day 29: Careless Words 134

Day 30: Take the High Road 138

Day 31: Guiding Lights 142

Day 32: Hearts Like Flowers 146

Day 33: New Horizons 150

Day 34: Guard the Gates 155

Day 35: Crushed 159

Day 36: By the Sea 164

Day 37: New Eyes to See 168

Day 38: Worn Down and Weary 172

Day 39: Get Moving 176

Day 40: A Life That Shines 180

Day 41: Rowing Together 185

Day 42: The Bitter and the Sweet 190

Day 43: A Cordial Welcome 195

Day 44: Generosity of Spirit 199

Day 45: To All Generations 203

Day 46: Dearer Every Minute 207

Day 47: A Bountiful Harvest 212

Father's Letter: While We Wait 217

An Invitation 221

Author's Note 223

Moments with Marmee: Words of Wisdom from Mrs. March . . .224

Acknowledgments 227

Bibliography 229

About the Author 231

A Little Women
WELCOME

I'll never forget the first time my mother put a copy of Louisa May Alcott's *Little Women* in my hands. She said, "You will love it, but it will make you cry."

And isn't that true? *Little Women* has warmed hearts for generations now—making us laugh, smile, *and* cry each time we read it. The story is sweet and tender, familiar and comforting. Even the names of the characters—Marmee, Meg, Jo, Beth, Amy, and Laurie—evoke vibrant memories. Opening the first few pages of *Little Women* feels like stepping in the front door of the March home and joining the cozy family circle by the fire.

When we think of the March family, nostalgic images of hearth and home immediately come to mind. We picture a snug house bursting with activity, plays and club meetings up in the garret, hymns around the piano by candlelight, and lively meals at the table. Most of all, we imagine a dear family that loves together, prays together, and believes together.

Though it was written long ago, *Little Women* still strikes a chord with readers today. Its relatable characters and themes stand the test of time. In it we read about family and friends, war and peace, work and calling, love and loss. We learn that hard work is good for us and a cheerful heart makes it more enjoyable. We discover that the key to contentment isn't found in having everything we want but in learning to make much of what we've been given.

Little Women is also a treasure trove of timeless spiritual themes. Many of its lessons and motifs are drawn from the Bible, *Pilgrim's Progress* by John Bunyan, and other Christian writings. In the March home, Christian morals are valued and practiced. Faith, hope, and love abound. Mr. March leads his family with loving care and patient kindness. Mrs. March ("Marmee") teaches and trains her daughters with tenderness and practical wisdom. The March sisters learn to pray, have personal devotions, and walk with God in their daily lives. And faith is at the center of it all.

Finally, *Little Women* shows us what it looks like to live in close community with other believers. In the March family—as in the family of God—everyone has a part to play and no one walks alone. As they work and live side by side, they soften each other's rough edges and sharpen one another as "iron sharpens iron" (Proverbs 27:17). They each use their unique gifts and talents to serve the Lord and others. They learn to care for their neighbors, comfort each other in their afflictions, hold fast to God's Word, walk in close relationship with Jesus, and invite others to gather with them around the fellowship table.

———◦◆◦———

You are holding this book in your hands for a reason. The Lord wants to meet with you and speak to you through His Word. As you spend time with Him each day, your faith will grow and flourish. God will direct your path, comfort you, and encourage you. Listen for His voice, and keep a notebook and a pen handy so you can take note of all you're learning. Press into Jesus, and allow Him to do a new work in your heart and life.

In this book, you'll find one devotional entry for every corresponding chapter of *Little Women*, each with key moments from that chapter of the novel, thoughts for personal reflection, selected Bible passages, and a short prayer. When you sit down to read, take time to prepare your heart. Invite the Holy Spirit to speak and move. Come to God with a posture to receive—hands open, head bowed, heart humble.

As you begin this journey, I invite you to curl up in a cozy spot and enjoy a nostalgic visit with the March family. There is so much God wants to do in your life. Things He wants to teach you and show you. Wounds He wants to heal. Places where He is calling you to serve. And a unique role for you to play in His kingdom. May your time reading this devotional inspire a new-found joy in the Lord, a greater passion for Jesus, and a deeper understanding of His plans and purposes for your life.

Day 1

BEGIN AGAIN IN EARNEST

—◦•◦—

Live a life worthy of the Lord and please him in every way: bearing fruit in every good work, growing in the knowledge of God.

COLOSSIANS 1:10 NIV

> "Now, my little pilgrims, suppose you begin again, not in play, but in earnest, and see how far on you can get before Father comes home."

[CHAPTER 1]

Little Women opens with Meg, Jo, Beth, and Amy by the fire, "knitting away in the twilight," sighing over a "Christmas without any presents," and lamenting the absence of Father, who is "far away, where the fighting is." They decide to buy gifts for themselves and "have a little fun," but when Beth sets Marmee's slippers on the hearth to warm, the "sight of the old shoes" has a "good effect upon the girls." They decide to spend their money on Marmee instead.

After supper the girls gather close around Marmee's chair to read a letter from Father and the special note he included for his "little girls at home." He says he thinks of them by day and prays for them by night. And he encourages them to use their time apart to "do their duty faithfully, fight their bosom enemies bravely, and conquer themselves so beautifully" that when he comes home, he may be "fonder and prouder than ever of [his] little women."

As the girls sniff back tears, Marmee reminds them of how they used to "play pilgrims" from *Pilgrim's Progress* as little girls. She inspires them to "begin again, not in play, but in earnest," now that they are older, and see how far they can get in their journey of faith before Father comes home. Delighted with the idea, they agree to try it and start making plans. Marmee tells them to look for their "guidebooks" under their pillows on Christmas morning.

Like the March sisters, we all are on a pilgrimage. As followers of Jesus Christ, this world is not our permanent home (Hebrews 13:14). But while we're here, we've been given important work to do: We each have a road to travel, burdens to carry, and weaknesses to overcome. We have people to love and duties to fulfill. And every day we have the opportunity to "begin again, not in play, but in earnest" on our journey toward loving Jesus more and pleasing Him in every way (Colossians 1:10).

In the New Testament, we find an inspiring picture of what it looks like to follow Jesus "in earnest." After Jesus ascended into heaven, His followers "devoted themselves to the apostles' teaching and the fellowship, to the breaking of bread and the prayers" (Acts 2:42 ESV). Each day, they attended services together at the temple and broke bread in their homes (Acts 2:46). And everywhere they went, they told people about Jesus. As a result, "the Lord added to their number day by day those who were being saved" (Acts 2:47 ESV).

> *Let us also lay aside every weight, and sin*
> *which clings so closely, and let us run with*
> *endurance the race that is set before us.*
> HEBREWS 12:1 ESV

PERSONAL APPLICATION:

Do you want to "begin again" in your walk with God? Is there something you've been "playing" at but now want to pursue "in earnest"? Maybe you want to grow in your daily devotions, join a Bible study, or find an accountability partner. Or perhaps you're ready to fully commit (or recommit) to following Jesus with all your heart.

God wants to do a new work in your life today! He is the God of new beginnings, revival, and renewal. Make it your prayer to "live a life worthy of the Lord and please him in every way: bearing fruit in every good work, growing in the knowledge of God" (Colossians 1:10 NIV). And if you've been trying to make this journey of faith on your own, join hands with your brothers and sisters in Christ. We all are pilgrims, and yet we are never alone.

PRAYER FOR TODAY:

Heavenly Father, I want to start fresh with You today. Please do a new work in me. I want to draw close to You and renew my commitment to follow You and love You all the days of my life. I give You my whole heart and soul. In those areas where I'm weary and need Your encouragement, please speak to my heart. I especially need Your strength to begin again in earnest in this area of my life: [your prayer]. In Jesus' name, amen.

"Love the Lord your God with all your heart and with all your soul and with all your strength and with all your mind."
LUKE 10:27 NIV

Day 2

THE LEAST
OF THESE

---

*"Truly I tell you, whatever you did for
one of the least of these brothers and
sisters of mine, you did for me."*

MATTHEW 25:40 NIV

> *And when they went away, leaving comfort behind, I think there were not in all the city four merrier people than the hungry little girls who gave away their breakfasts and contented themselves with bread and milk on Christmas morning.*
>
> [CHAPTER 2]

Jo finds "a little crimson-covered book" under her pillow on Christmas morning—a copy of "that beautiful old story of the best life ever lived." It's described as a "true guidebook for any pilgrim going on a long journey."[1] Meg's copy is green, Beth's is dove, and Amy's is blue, each with "the same picture inside, and a few words written by their mother." Meg suggests that they "read a little every morning," a habit they've "neglected" since their lives were "unsettled" when Father went away. And they all settle down to read quietly for a half hour.

At breakfast their faith is quickly put to the test. As they prepare to eat the beautiful breakfast Hannah cooked and give their gifts to Marmee, Mrs. March comes in from visiting a "poor woman with a little newborn baby" and six hungry children "huddled into one bed to keep from freezing." She asks if they will give the Hummel family their breakfast as a Christmas present,

---

1 Amy's book is later referred to as a "testament" (ch. 19); thus, it's likely that these "guidebooks" as personal copies of *The New Testament*, though some readers believe they are copies of *Pilgrim's Progress* by John Bunyan.

and after a short pause, the four sisters quickly pack up their delicious feast.

At the Hummel home, they see things they've never encountered: "A poor, bare, miserable room. . .with broken windows, no fire, ragged bedclothes, a sick mother, wailing baby, and a group of pale, hungry children cuddled under one old quilt." They set to work quickly, building up the fire, caring for the mother, and feeding the children. Afterward Meg says, "That's loving our neighbor better than ourselves, and I like it."

The March sisters give away their breakfast and content "themselves with bread and milk," leaving "comfort behind" them. And the result is this: "there were not in all the city four merrier people." Haven't you found that to be true? When we give away our best, we come away with merry hearts! It's easier to give away our milk and bread instead of our "cakes and cream and. . .muffings" [sic], but it's a true sacrifice of praise to give away what we cherish most.

When you love and care for others, you show kindness to Jesus Himself. Jesus said, "I was hungry and you gave me something to eat, I was thirsty and you gave me something to drink, I was a stranger and you invited me in, I needed clothes and you clothed me, I was sick and you looked after me, I was in prison and you came to visit me" (Matthew 25:35–36 NIV). If you're wondering how you can possibly do any of those things for Jesus, Jesus explained it like this: "Truly I tell you, whatever you did for one of the least of these brothers and sisters of mine, you did for me" (Matthew 25:40 NIV).

And do not forget to do good and to share with others, for with such sacrifices God is pleased.
HEBREWS 13:16 NIV

PERSONAL APPLICATION:

Where can you "leave comfort behind" you in your daily life? What can you do in your home, in your neighborhood, or at your office or school to bring comfort to others? Ask God to show you how you can use your gifts to bless and love your neighbor as yourself today (Mark 12:31).

The March girls start their day with morning devotions, something they've neglected since "father went away" and the war "unsettled them". If they hadn't spent that first half hour of the day preparing their hearts, they might not have so cheerfully given their breakfast away. Do you have a time and a tucked-away place for your personal devotions? If not, think of ways to make that time special and make it a priority.

———◦◆◦———

PRAYER FOR TODAY:

Thank You, Lord, for this reminder to prepare my heart through Bible reading and prayer each day. Please help me look for ways to love my neighbor, bless my family and friends, and leave comfort behind me wherever I go this week. When I am too focused on my own comfort, help me see other people's needs. Show me how I can bless these people today: [specific names]. In Jesus' name, amen.

A generous person will prosper; whoever refreshes others will be refreshed.
PROVERBS 11:25 NIV

Day 3

BURNT CURLS AND BALLROOM TWIRLS

———◇◆◇———

*I praise you, for I am fearfully
and wonderfully made.*
PSALM 139:14 ESV

Jo March isn't like most girls her age. She's clumsy and awkward and "never trouble[s] herself much about dress." She doesn't "care much for company dancing" and would rather "fly about and cut capers." On the night of the New Year's Eve dance, her dress is torn and burnt, her gloves are stained, and when she tries to curl Meg's hair, she accidentally burns it off. At the dance, Jo spills coffee on her front and spoils Meg's white glove mopping it up.

While Meg makes friends and is asked to dance, Jo feels "as much out of place as a colt in a flower garden." However, when she slips into a "curtained recess, intending to peep and enjoy herself in peace," she bumps into Laurie and they make a party of their own. They dance a "grand polka" in the hall, and then when Meg sprains her ankle, they have a "merry time" over tea, "bonbons and mottoes," and a game of "Buzz" with "two or three other young people."

Jo March may not shine in a ballroom, but she has her own unique niche in the world. Her favorite "refuge" is the garret, where she can curl up with a comforter on the "old three-legged sofa," eating apples and crying over a good book. She loves to read, write, play, and "tramp." She's a wonderful sister, friend, and daughter. She's loyal and loving, brave and forthright. And we can't imagine the March family without her in it.

Don't you love Jo for being Jo? God feels the same way about you. He made you with a special purpose in mind, and He has given you gifts, talents, and interests that line up with the work He has planned for you to do. He has fitted you for the place where He has you today—in your family, in your friendships, and in your church. And while it's good to push past your comfort zone and try new things, there are certain areas where you're best suited to work and serve. It often takes time and persistence to find your niche, but if you pay attention and listen carefully, God will lead you to places where you can blossom and bloom.

In the New Testament, God used Priscilla and Aquila, a husband-and-wife tent-making team, to creatively share the Gospel. They helped Paul with his ministry (Romans 16:3), risked their lives for the Gospel (Romans 16:4), hosted a home church (Romans 16:5), and helped train Apollos (Acts 18:26). God didn't choose highly educated theologians or eloquent orators to grow the Church; He chose two people who were great at making tents and had a passion for daily, personal ministry.

For we are his workmanship, created in
Christ Jesus for good works, which God prepared
beforehand, that we should walk in them.
EPHESIANS 2:10 ESV

PERSONAL APPLICATION:

Where do you feel most comfortable? What do you love to do? God can use all of your talents and interests for His kingdom and His glory. You don't have to be the best, the brightest, or the most educated to be used by God. Whether you're young or old, go to school or work, stay at home or care for others, you can encourage hearts, plant seeds for the Gospel, and help teach people how to follow Jesus.

Meg, Jo, Beth, and Amy were *very* different from one another, but they each contributed something wonderful and necessary to their family and home. As you serve Jesus in your little corner of the world, do it wholeheartedly. Commit everything to the Lord, and ask Him to do a work in and through you. You might be surprised at what happens next!

———◦◆◦———

PRAYER FOR TODAY:

Lord God, I believe You made me for a purpose. Please show me how I can serve You with my skills and interests. Open my eyes to ways I can share Your love with others in my own unique way. Speak to my heart and direct my paths. Show me the good work You have for me to do today, and help me serve the people around me with the gifts You have given. Please help me resist the temptation to be like other people. Teach me to embrace Your design for my life in this area: [your request]. In Jesus' name, amen.

As each has received a gift, use it to serve one another, as good stewards of God's varied grace.
1 PETER 4:10 ESV

Day 4

A CURE FOR THE GRUMPS

Rejoice always, pray without ceasing,
give thanks in all circumstances.
1 Thessalonians 5:16–18 esv

> [Jo and Meg] always looked back before turning the corner, for their mother was always at the window to nod and smile, and wave her hand to them.
>
> [CHAPTER 4]

One morning when the holidays are over and the "week of merrymaking" is done, everyone in the March household seems "rather out of sorts and inclined to croak." Jo and Meg prepare to go off into the cold winter day to jobs they dislike, Beth has a headache on the sofa, and Amy frets over her school lessons. Even Hannah has "the grumps," and Marmee is distracted as she rushes to finish a letter.

"There never was such a cross family!" cries Jo, who loses her temper and spills the ink, breaks her boot laces, and sits on her hat. Everyone is at odds with one another, scolding, imploring, wailing, and complaining. The two eldest leave for work with Hannah's hot turnovers in their pockets, grumbling as they go. But as they turn at the corner to look back, there's Marmee at the window—"like sunshine"—waving to them like always.

That evening by the fire, they all tell stories from their day and start to cheer up. Marmee talks about a man she met who had suffered many losses in his family. She says his story made her realize something important: "I had all my girls to comfort me at home, and his last son was waiting, miles away, to say good-by to him, perhaps! I felt so rich, so happy thinking of my blessings." Everyone's mood softens, and the girls make up their minds to "stop complaining" and "enjoy [their] blessings."

It *is* hard to "take up our packs" on days when we're tired, out of sorts, or don't like the jobs we have to do. But a little bit of perspective goes a long way when we consider the plight of others and start to notice all the things we've been given. When we turn our focus from the mess in front of us to the hope that's before us, our whole attitude shifts. As we choose thankfulness, everything changes.

When Paul and Silas were beaten and put into jail, it must have been terrible (Acts 16). Imagine sitting in chains in a dirty first-century jail, with painful bruises and cuts all over your body from being stripped and beaten (v. 22). Most of us would probably moan and cry all evening or possibly be enraged by the injustice, but they spent the evening praying and singing hymns (v. 25). What happened next is incredible: the doors of the jail opened, their chains fell off, and the jailer and his whole family accepted Christ and got baptized!

Sing and make music from your heart to the Lord,
always giving thanks to God the Father for
everything, in the name of our Lord Jesus Christ.
EPHESIANS 5:19–20 NIV

PERSONAL APPLICATION:

We've all had days like the March family when everyone has "the grumps" and nothing goes right. In those moments it helps to take a deep breath, raise our heads, and look up. If we remember we're on the same team, it makes a difference! And when we start praising God—even for the tiniest things—our spirits rise. We begin to notice blessings in unlikely places and find joy in the details.

Two things change the tone of the day for Jo and Meg as they go out the door: Hannah makes hot turnovers for them even though she's tired, and Marmee stands to smile and wave at the window, sending "sunshine" with them. Perhaps you can find a way to share a little cheer with your family members, roommates, or coworkers this week. It could be a handwritten note, help with an errand, or a basket of warm muffins.

PRAYER FOR TODAY:

Lord, thank You for all the little blessings you shower me with each day. Help me to notice your gifts in the details of my life. When I feel overwhelmed, grumpy, and out of sorts, remind me to look up and take a moment to pray. Help me exchange my grumbling for gratitude. May I be a light that shines for You in the lives of others. Show me how I can help brighten this person's day today: [specific name]. In Jesus' name, amen.

Give thanks to the LORD, for he is good;
his love endures forever.
PSALM 118:1 NIV

Day 5

MEET THE
NEIGHBORS

*Let each of you look not only to his own interests,
but also to the interests of others.*

PHILIPPIANS 2:4 ESV

> "Here I am, bag and baggage,"
> [Jo] said briskly. "Mother sent
> her love, and was glad if I could
> do anything for you."
> [CHAPTER 5]

One winter day, Jo decides to make friends with "the Laurence boy," who looks "as if he would like to be known, if he only knew how to begin." She thinks he's "suffering for society and fun" and throws a snowball at his window to start the conversation. She is soon invited up and agrees to come "if Mother will let" her. She arrives, "looking rosy and quite at her ease, with a covered dish in one hand and Beth's three kittens in the other."

Meg's pretty blancmange is set aside for teatime, and the kittens from Beth help Laurie forget his "bashfulness." Jo looks around the room and decides to "right it up in two minutes" by brushing the hearth, straightening the mantelpiece, arranging Laurie's books and bottles, turning the sofa away from the light, and plumping the pillows. After she has "whisked things into place and given quite a different air to the room," they settle in for a chat.

As they talk, Jo quickly realizes Laurie is "sick and lonely." She sees "how rich" she is in "home and happiness" and wants to "share it with him." She listens as he confesses to watching her family through the window in the evening "when the lamps are lighted," and she notices the twitch in his lips when he mentions having no mother of his own. In that moment Jo decides to invite Laurie into their lives and make him part of her family.

When Jo steps in and befriends Laurie, she brings light and life into his otherwise lonely, dull life. It's a beautiful thing when neighbors—people who live, work, study, or serve side by side—take an interest in one another and share each other's burdens. The moment someone notices our difficulties and kindly pushes their way into our lives, it's a blessed relief. We can all get stuck in our routines or too focused on our own set of woes, and sometimes we need someone to march in and "right it up."

During His time here, Jesus walked into lives, houses, and messes every day without blinking an eye. He ate with tax collectors and sinners (Mark 2:16) and healed blind, lame, and leprous people. He sat and talked with the Samaritan woman at the well even though He knew every sinful thing she ever did (John 4). Everywhere He went, Jesus invited people to repent of their sins and enter into God's kingdom of light. And He has done the same for you. Jesus stepped into your life at just the right moment—to invite you to enjoy the riches of His Father's family forever.

God sets the lonely in families.
PSALM 68:6 NIV

PERSONAL APPLICATION:

What do you have that you can share with others? In what ways are you "rich in home and happiness?" Many people, like Laurie, would like to be known but don't know where to begin. There are neighbors who need visiting, parents who need sitters, teachers who need encouragement, pastors who need prayer, and friends who need cheering up. Small tokens of kindness make a big impact when someone is going through a rough patch.

The "bag and baggage" we share with others doesn't have to be fancy. A small treat, a kind word, or a simple prayer can go a long way. Often the very fact that you take the time to show you care is enough. Your presence speaks volumes to that friend or neighbor who feels alone, anxious, or forgotten. Keep your eyes open this week for someone who might need a friendly visit or a tight hug.

PRAYER FOR TODAY:

Dearest Jesus, thank You for loving me so well and for coming into my life when I needed You most. I was lonely, lost, and without comfort, and You came in and brought me joy and great spiritual riches. Please help me to truly see the people around me and find ways to step into their lives and build friendships. Make a way for me to invite this person to know You more: [specific name]. In Jesus' name, amen.

---

*Do not neglect to show hospitality to strangers,
for thereby some have entertained angels unawares.*
HEBREWS 13:2 ESV

Day 6

MAKING MUSIC
WITH OUR LIVES

Let no one seek his own good,
but the good of his neighbor.

1 CORINTHIANS 10:24 ESV

> *The big house did prove a Palace Beautiful, though it took some time for all to get in, and Beth found it very hard to pass the lions.*
>
> [CHAPTER 6]

Jo's neighborly advances bless everyone involved: "Such plays and tableaux, such sleigh rides and skating frolics, such pleasant evenings in the old parlor, and now and then such gay little parties at the great house." Laurie enjoys "Mrs. March's motherly welcome" and the "innocent companionship" of the "simple-hearted girls." With Mr. Laurence's invitation, Meg can now "walk in the conservatory," Jo can browse in "the new library voraciously," and Amy can copy pictures "to her heart's content."

However, shy Beth finds it particularly hard to "pass the lion" and enter the "Palace Beautiful" to play the grand piano next door. But when Mr. Laurence says she "needn't see or speak to anyone, but run in at any time," she is overjoyed. It takes "two or three retreats" before Beth finally plucks up her courage to go over and walk in the side door. From then on, her "little brown hood" is seen slipping through the hedge to play the piano "nearly every day."

Beth enjoys herself "heartily," but there's a double blessing when she goes next door. Mr. Laurence finds great comfort in her playing and quietly opens "his study door to hear." New music appears on the rack, and Laurie keeps the servants away. And when Beth makes slippers for Mr. Laurence, he sends over a little cabinet piano, "which once belonged to the little grand daughter he lost." Beth thanks him with a hug and a kiss and sits on his knee to talk. It's the beginning of a tender friendship for both.

When Beth brings music back into the house next door, she also unknowingly ushers in personal healing and comfort for Mr. Laurence. We each have a kind of "music" we make with our lives. There is a tune and tone to your life that God can use to open doors and hearts. When you take brave steps of faith and do the things God has created you to do, it often proves mutually beneficial. Not only do you personally grow and flourish, but the people around you experience joy and blessing as well.

This is especially true in the body of Christ. When we use our spiritual gifts, we help build up the Church for the common good of all (1 Corinthians 12:7). When we hang back, we delay our own growth and hold on to the very things that might help the people around us most. Scripture says this: "God has given each of you a gift from his great variety of spiritual gifts. Use them well to serve one another" (1 Peter 4:10 NLT). As we exercise our gifts accordingly, with passion and enthusiasm, the whole body grows and flourishes.

Now to each one the manifestation of
the Spirit is given for the common good.
1 CORINTHIANS 12:7 NIV

PERSONAL APPLICATION:

Is there a door God is asking you to be brave and knock on? A place where He is calling you to serve? Whatever your gifting, whether it's teaching, helping, encouraging, organizing, managing, comforting, counseling, or making music, take a step of faith today and ask God how you can serve Him with those gifts.

What kind of music do you make with your life? If you prefer a quiet home life, private pursuits, and serving behind the scenes, God can use that to create a comforting and peaceful space for people who are worn and weary. If you are outgoing, adventurous, and bold, God can use you to step into places other people might avoid. Rest assured, He can use *your* unique blend of personality and giftings to build up other believers and help make disciples.

———◦◆◦———

PRAYER FOR TODAY:

Lord Jesus, thank You for showing me that I have a part to play in the lives of the people around me. Please help me to understand how You've made me and how I can serve you. Show me how to take steps of faith in places where I'm timid and unsure, and help me make music for others in the way I live and love. Teach me how to use my gifts and talents in this area: [your prayer]. In Jesus' name, amen.

For it is God who works in you, both to will and to work for his good pleasure.
PHILIPPIANS 2:13 ESV

Day 7
PICKLED LIMES AND BITTER TIMES

Pride leads to disgrace,
but with humility comes wisdom.
PROVERBS 11:2 NLT

> *To others it might seem a ludicrous or trivial affair, but to [Amy] it was a hard experience.*
>
> [CHAPTER 7]

In this chapter Amy's pilgrimage takes her through the "Valley of Humiliation." When she's caught with pickled limes in her desk, she receives "several tingling blows on her little palm" and a major blow to her pride. Though the slaps were "neither many nor heavy," we are told it made "no difference to her" because for the "first time in her life she had been struck, and the disgrace, in her eyes, was as deep as if he had knocked her down."

For others, Amy's situation might seem "a ludicrous or trivial affair," but to her it's a "hard experience." She has never faced anything like it before; her upbringing has been "governed by love alone." As she's forced to stand in front of the class until recess, "the proud and sensitive little girl" suffers a "shame and pain which she never forgot." The sting on her hand is nothing compared to the embarrassment she feels because she knows her family will be "disappointed."

At home Marmee says she wouldn't have chosen the teacher's "way of mending a fault," but she thinks it still might help teach Amy an important lesson. She shares a hard truth with Amy: "You are getting to be rather conceited, my dear, and it is quite time you set about correcting it. You have a good many little gifts and virtues, but there is no need of parading them, for conceit spoils the finest genius."

We've all experienced humiliating moments like Amy—moments that teach us hard lessons we won't soon forget. Pride is easy to spot and point out in others, but it's extremely hard to diagnose in ourselves. It convinces us that we're right, that our feelings are justified, that we deserve better, that our way is best. When we receive a correction, it's what we do with it that matters. We can dig in our heels, deny the issue, and defend ourselves, or we can humble our hearts and ask God to open our eyes and ears to what we need to see and hear.

King David knew firsthand about hidden blind spots and undetected pride. When he committed adultery with Bathsheba and had her husband killed, the prophet Nathan went and confronted David (2 Samuel 12). He wasn't afraid to tell David the truth—that he had stolen another man's wife and committed murder. The truth hurt, but it was the best thing for David; it unblinded his eyes, brought him to confession and repentance, and restored him to God.

Create in me a pure heart, O God,
and renew a steadfast spirit within me.
PSALM 51:10 NIV

PERSONAL APPLICATION:

Where do you see pride at work in your life? It's subtle and comes in various forms, so it's vital that we open ourselves up to the Lord and to honest, loving friends on a regular basis. Praying Psalm 139:23–24 (NIV) is a wonderful way to combat problematic blind spots: "Search me, God, and know my heart; test me and know my anxious thoughts. See if there is any offensive way in me, and lead me in the way everlasting."

If you're in a situation that seems like a "ludicrous or trivial affair" to others but is a "hard experience" for you, be assured that it's not trivial to the Lord. Perhaps you've been wronged, humiliated, or embarrassed by someone. Maybe you received a correction that wasn't given in love or was done at the wrong time or place. Ask the Lord to teach you lessons from the situation and to help you move forward with grace and humility.

PRAYER FOR TODAY:

Thank You, Jesus, for reminding me of my blind spots and those areas that need refinement. It's embarrassing when I'm in the wrong, but please help me humble myself, ask forgiveness, and mend my ways. I ask You to search my heart and show me any hidden pride or lurking sin. Please create in me a clean heart in this area of my life: [your prayer]. In Jesus' name, amen.

> "For all those who exalt themselves
> will be humbled, and those who humble
> themselves will be exalted."
>
> LUKE 14:11 NIV

Day 8

THE SINCEREST PRAYER

*Let us then approach God's throne of grace with
confidence, so that we may receive mercy and
find grace to help us in our time of need.*
HEBREWS 4:16 NIV

> [Jo drew] nearer to the Friend who always welcomes every child with a love stronger than that of any father, tenderer than that of any mother.
>
> [CHAPTER 8]

When Jo and Amy argue one evening, Amy gets her revenge in the worst possible way—by burning the little book of fairy tales Jo wrote, the "loving work of several years." Filled with anger and grief over the "dreadful calamity," Jo shakes Amy until her teeth chatter, saying, "You wicked, wicked girl! I never can write it again, and I'll never forgive you as long as I live."

The next day, Jo's anger builds into a "bitter, unhappy sort of satisfaction in her sister's troubles." In fact, we're told she "cherished her anger till it grew strong and took possession of her." It's only when Amy falls through the ice while skating on the river that Jo's heart melts. She realizes that her anger almost cost her something much more precious than her stories. Once Amy is safe and warm and asleep by the fire, Jo falls down beside Marmee in "a passion of penitent tears. . .bitterly condemning her hardness of heart, and sobbing out her gratitude."

In a tender conversation, Jo and Marmee talk together about their quick tempers. Jo says it feels like she could "do anything" when she's angry, that she gets "so savage" she could "hurt anyone and enjoy it."

Marmee gives Jo this advice: "Watch and pray, dear, never get tired of trying, and never think it is impossible to conquer your fault." She teaches Jo that she can "overcome and outlive" all her "troubles and temptations" if she can learn to "feel the strength and tenderness of [her] Heavenly Father" through prayer:

> *The more you love and trust Him, the nearer you*
> *will feel to Him, and the less you will depend on*
> *human power and wisdom. His love and care*
> *never tire or change, can never be taken from you,*
> *but may become the source of lifelong peace,*
> *happiness, and strength. Believe this heartily,*
> *and go to God with all your little cares, and hopes,*
> *and sins, and sorrows, as freely and confidingly as*
> *you come to your mother.*

Jo snuggles close to Marmee and prays "the sincerest prayer she had ever prayed," drawing "nearer to the Friend who always welcomes every child with a love stronger than that of any father, tenderer than that of any mother."

This chapter brings up several important questions: How *do* we forgive people when they hurt us deeply? And what can we do when our anger threatens to overtake us? We've all experienced wounds from others. There are memories we can't seem to shake, pain we struggle to release. However, when we "cherish" our anger, allowing it to grow and take possession of us, it can quickly burn out of control. Bitterness takes roots and slowly eats away at us, causing even more damage to ourselves and others. The only road to true healing starts with forgiveness.

Jesus gave His life for the unpardonable, unforgivable sins of this world. He died for every single person's sin in all of history, including yours and mine. Jesus set the example for how to forgive people who hurt us. He even asked His Father to "forgive" the men who murdered Him—He who had done nothing deserving of death—by nailing Him to a cross (Luke 23:34). And He said this to His followers: "If you forgive those who sin against you, your heavenly Father will forgive you" (Matthew 6:14 NLT).

Be kind to one another, tenderhearted,
forgiving one another, as God in Christ forgave you.
EPHESIANS 4:32 ESV

PERSONAL APPLICATION:

We all feel rather "savage" at times and struggle to control our thoughts, words, and emotions. But instead of running away or hiding from God in the face of fierce temptation, run *toward* Him. God hears your "sincerest" prayers. When you're at your worst, Jesus is at His best. In your weakness, His power is made perfect (2 Corinthians 12:9).

Do you know the "strength and tenderness" of your heavenly Father? Take this time to watch and pray, bringing all your "faults"—your bitterness, your temper, your unforgiveness, your temptations, your jealousy, your pride—to your Father who loves you. Never get tired of trying. Nothing is impossible with God! Remember that you have "a better Friend" who is always by your side to "comfort and sustain" you.

PRAYER FOR TODAY:

Lord, thank You for dying for me and for forgiving all my sins. I confess that my hurt and anger can quickly turn into bitterness and hardness of heart. Teach me to control my temper and resist temptation. I especially ask for Your grace to forgive the deeper wounds I carry, the people who never apologized, the words that I can't unhear. Please heal my heart and help me to forgive these people in particular: [specific names].
In Jesus' name, amen.

When the righteous cry for help, the LORD hears and delivers them out of all their troubles.
PSALM 34:17 ESV

Day 9
ALL DOLLED UP

❧—◆—❧

Godliness with contentment is great gain.
1 Timothy 6:6 esv

> "Well, I am happy, and I won't fret, but it does seem as if the more one gets the more one wants, doesn't it?"
>
> [CHAPTER 9]

When Meg visits the Moffats' "fashionable" home, she is struck with envy over Annie Moffat's finery and riches. She allows herself to be dressed up "in style" and made into "a fine lady." At an evening party, with her "long skirts trailing, her earrings tinkling, her curls waving," she finds that her "borrowed plumes" attract a new "class of people." When Laurie tries to talk sense to her, she says, "I'm not Meg tonight, I'm 'a doll' who does all sorts of crazy things."

Meg dances, flirts, chatters, and giggles, drinks too much, and ends up feeling like she "hadn't enjoyed herself as much as she expected." She's sick all the next day and goes home early because she's so worn out. At home she tells her family all about the "charming time she had," but after the younger girls go to bed, she "fesses" to Marmee and Jo about everything else—the drinking, the flirting, the gossip, and her love of being "praised and admired."

As they talk Marmee shares her hopes and prayers for her daughters, that they might be "beautiful, accomplished, and good" and "admired, loved, and respected." She wants them to have "a happy youth," be "well and wisely married," and lead "useful, pleasant lives, with as little care and sorrow to try them as God sees fit to send." Furthermore, she says she'd rather they were poor as long as they are "happy, beloved, [and] contented."

Psalm 34:10 (NIV) says, "Those who seek the LORD lack no good thing." Sometimes it feels like we *do* lack something good that we need or want. Often our hearts ache over loss, disappointment, and shattered dreams. But in Philippians 4:19 (NIV), God promises to meet *all* our needs "according to the riches of his glory in Christ Jesus." God dearly cares for you and is tending to your needs right now, even if you can't see it. He is your shelter, your comfort, and your security.

Discontentment goes all the way back to the garden of Eden, where Adam and Eve had everything they needed, including all they could eat and perfect fellowship with God. But when Eve "*saw* that the fruit of the tree was good for food and *pleasing to the eye*, and also *desirable for gaining wisdom*, she took some and ate it" (Genesis 3:6 NIV, emphasis mine). In that moment Eve fell for the same lie Satan continues to tell today—that God is withholding good things from us. But the real truth is this: sometimes God withholds things for our good.

> *Those who seek the*
> *LORD lack no good thing.*
> PSALM 34:10 NIV

PERSONAL APPLICATION:

What are the desires of your heart? Maybe you ache for a loving spouse, children of your own, or a close group of friends. Or perhaps you long for better health, a solid home church, or stronger family relationships. All of these desires are *good*, but if they become your main goal, things can get out of balance. Focus your attention on the lovely people and provisions God has given you for today, and ask Him to fill you with peace.

Marmee's final advice is this: "Make this home happy, so that you may be fit for homes of your own, if they are offered you, and contented here if they are not." Let this be an invitation for you today. Concentrate on making your current situation as happy as it can be. Prepare your heart for what might come next, but practice contentment right where God has you now.

PRAYER FOR TODAY:

Thank You, Father, for providing for all my needs. I confess that I sometimes find myself longing for what I don't have. Show me what I need to surrender at Your feet and where I need to be patient. Help me trust You to work all things for good in my life. I want to grow in contentment and cultivate a life of faithfulness, not a habit of always wanting more. Please speak to my heart about my discontentment in this part of my life: [your prayer]. In Jesus' name, amen.

For the Lord God is a sun and shield; the Lord bestows favor and honor. No good thing does he withhold from those who walk uprightly.

Psalm 84:11 esv

Day 10

MAKE ROOM
FOR MORE

"I was a stranger and you invited me in."
MATTHEW 25:35 NIV

> *No one ever regretted the admittance of Sam Weller, for a more devoted, well-behaved, and jovial member no club could have.*
>
> [CHAPTER 10]

In chapter 10 we're introduced to the March sisters' Dickensian Pickwick Club (P.C.), an exclusive secret society, with Meg as Samuel Pickwick, Jo as Augustus Snodgrass, Beth as Tracy Tupman, and Amy as Nathaniel Winkle. They meet in the garret to go over club business and read the *Pickwick Portfolio*, their weekly newspaper, which is "filled with original tales, poetry, local news, funny advertisements, and hints."

The meeting starts out quite happily, until Jo asks the P.C. to admit Laurie as a new member: "I wish to propose the admission of a new member—one who highly deserves the honor, would be deeply grateful for it, and would add immensely to the spirit of the club, the literary value of the paper, and be no end jolly and nice." They take a vote, with Jo and Beth saying "Aye" and Meg and Amy being "contrary-minded."

Amy says boys "only joke and bounce about" and insists the P.C. is "a ladies' club" that is "private and proper." Meg thinks Laurie will laugh at their newspaper and make fun of them. But Jo wins them over with this: "We can do so little for him, and he does so much for us, I think the least we can do is to offer him a place here, and make him welcome if he comes." With a vow of eternal devotion to the club and the gift of a post office "as a means of promoting friendly relations between adjoining nations," Laurie becomes a "devoted, well-behaved, and jovial" member of their club.

Making room for others and welcoming people into our homes, our family gatherings, our church groups, and our circles of friends is exactly what Jesus asks us to do as His followers. Jesus wants us to invite more people to know Him and love Him and be part of God's family forever. It's sometimes difficult to share your faith if you've never done it before. And it can be hard to break the ice with a new person. But as you make a habit of sharing your faith and building relationships, your life will be enriched by the people God brings your way.

The Bible says we were once "far off" from God, but we have now been "brought near by the blood of Christ" (Ephesians 2:13 NIV). Jesus wants "*all* people to be saved and to come to a knowledge of the truth" (1 Timothy 2:4 NIV, emphasis mine). In Romans 10:14 (NLT), Paul asked, "And how can they believe in him if they have never heard about him?" Jesus said, "The harvest is plentiful, but the laborers are few" (Matthew 9:37 ESV). Will you join Jesus in the harvest fields and invite people to know Him?

> *"Go into all the world and preach
> the Good News to everyone."*
> MARK 16:15 NLT

PERSONAL APPLICATION:

Take a moment to think about the people who invited you into their lives and helped you know and follow Jesus. Aren't you so glad they did that? Now it's your turn! Personal evangelism doesn't have to be fancy. It can start with a simple invitation to join you for coffee. As you build relationships and take a genuine interest in people's lives, ask the Holy Spirit to open the door for conversations about Jesus.

God's family is not an exclusive club. There are no membership fees or yearly dues. Salvation is a free gift through faith in Jesus. If you want to know Jesus as your personal Lord and Savior, you can do that today by simply asking Him to forgive your sins and come into your heart forever. For a sample prayer, please see "An Invitation" on page 221.

PRAYER FOR TODAY:

Lord, thank You for this beautiful picture of how wonderful it is when I invite people into my life and activities. Thank You for the many times You sent people to make me feel welcome. Help me connect with someone who needs a friend this week. Please give me the courage to say hello to someone new. I especially need Your help inviting people into this part of my life: [your prayer]. In Jesus' name, amen.

Therefore welcome one another as Christ has welcomed you, for the glory of God.
ROMANS 15:7 ESV

Day 11

LOUNGING AND LARKING

*Lazy people want much but get little,
but those who work hard will prosper.*
PROVERBS 13:4 NLT

> "*Lounging and larking doesn't pay,*"
> *observed Jo, shaking her head.*
> "*I'm tired of it and mean to go to*
> *work at something right off.*"
> [CHAPTER 11]

In this chapter the March sisters take a week off from their household chores. Meg wants to "rest and revel" to her "heart's content," Jo decides to read and enjoy "larks" with Laurie, and Amy and Beth put aside their lessons to "play all the time and rest." Marmee lets them try their "experiment" for a week to see how they "like it," saying by Saturday night they'll find "that all play and no work is as bad as all work and no play."

They begin the experiment "merrily" by "lounging" for the rest of the day, but as the week goes on, each sister finds herself with more troubles than she expected. None of them will "own" that they're "tired of the experiment," but they're glad when Friday comes. In a final moment of genius, Mrs. March gives Hannah "a holiday" on Saturday and takes a "vacation" day herself to show her girls "what happens when everyone thinks only of herself."

Saturday is the hardest day of all, with scrapes and heartache and everything going wrong. When Marmee comes home at the end of the day, she asks, "You think then, that it is better to have a few duties and live a little for others, do you?" Jo admits that "lounging and larking doesn't pay" and says she wants to "go to work at something right off." In the end the girls agree with Marmee's wisdom: "Work is wholesome, and there is plenty for everyone."

Do you have "regular hours for work and play"? Some of us are more prone to be all work and no play, while others of us may like to play more than we work. Wherever you fall on that spectrum, think carefully about finding a balance of the two. It always sounds wonderful to take a break and have nothing to do, but there's something built into us that needs order, purpose, and forward motion to keep us motivated and healthy.

The Bible gives us instructions for how to live and work, play and rest. In Colossians 3:23 (ESV) we read, "Whatever you do, work heartily, as for the Lord and not for men." Proverbs 14:23 (NIV) tells us, "All hard work brings a profit." And Ecclesiastes 9:10 (ESV) says, "Whatever your hand finds to do, do it with your might." Above all, we're exhorted to take every opportunity to share our faith with others, "in season and out of season," wherever our days take us (2 Timothy 4:2 NASB).

Whoever works his land will have plenty of bread,
but he who follows worthless pursuits lacks sense.
PROVERBS 12:11 ESV

PERSONAL APPLICATION:

Lounging and larking don't pay, but God *has* ordained one day a week to rest. Are you taking advantage of it? We're told to work hard for six days each week and commit the seventh day to the Lord (Exodus 20:8). If you believe that the other Ten Commandments are for your good and should be obeyed, then make it a priority to keep your Sabbath day holy.

Sabbath rest is a spiritual discipline that sadly goes unheeded by many Christians today. Burnout, strain, stress, and overwork are often the result. Look at your weekly schedule, and set aside a day for your Sabbath. You can pick the day, but guard it well. The enemy, the world, and your flesh will try to keep you from the refreshment and refueling you need. Prepare beforehand as much as possible, and make your Sabbath special. It's a gift!

PRAYER FOR TODAY:

Lord Jesus, thank You for today's reminder about rest and work. I need Your help to find a good balance between working diligently and setting aside my work for prayer, Bible reading, and quiet time. It's hard for me to be still and sit in Your presence, and I confess I don't always keep the Sabbath. Please help me grow in this area of work and play: [your prayer]. In Jesus' name, amen.

"Remember the Sabbath day by keeping it holy. Six days you shall labor and do all your work, but the seventh day is a sabbath to the Lord your God."
EXODUS 20:8–10 NIV

Day 12

PIN IT TO
YOUR HEART

—◦•◦—

*For sin will have no dominion over you,
since you are not under law but under grace.*
ROMANS 6:14 ESV

> "That does me good! That's worth millions of money and pecks of praise. Oh, Marmee, I do try! I will keep on trying, and not get tired, since I have you to help me."
>
> [CHAPTER 12]

When Fred Vaughn cheats at croquet at Camp Laurence, Jo's "quick temper" is tested. She dearly wants "to say something rude," but she checks "herself in time" and keeps silent. She remains "among the nettles" long enough to overcome her rage and comes back "looking cool and quiet." Laurie whispers, "Good for you, Jo!" And Meg says, "You kept your temper, and I'm so glad." Jo wins the game "by a clever stroke," but the real victory is the one she wins over her temper.

When Fred gives his ball "a sly nudge with his toe," Jo doesn't *feel* cool and quiet on the inside. She wants to "box his ears" and "boil over." But something helps her "hold" her tongue and "bite" her lip. That extra ounce of strength Jo needs comes from a well-timed note of encouragement she received earlier that morning from Marmee. Jo has it pinned "inside her frock, as a shield and a reminder," lest she be "taken unaware." It says,

I write a little word to tell you with how much satisfaction I watch your efforts to control your temper. You say nothing about your trials, failures, or successes, and think, perhaps, that no one sees

*them but the Friend whose help you daily ask, if I
may trust the well-worn cover of your guidebook. I,
too, have seen them all, and heartily believe in the
sincerity of your resolution, since it begins to bear
fruit. Go on, dear, patiently and bravely, and always
believe that no one sympathizes more tenderly with
you than your loving. . .[m]other.*

Marmee's note makes Jo's "cheeks glow and her eyes fill."
She says, "That does me good!" Laying "her head on her arms,"
she sheds a few "happy tears" because she thought "no one
saw and appreciated her efforts." The note is "doubly precious,
doubly encouraging" because it is "unexpected and from the
person whose commendation" Jo values most.

There is nothing quite like an unexpected word of encouragement just when we need it most. It can make our cheeks
glow and our eyes fill. Why? Because we all need support in our
trials and temptations. We often feel as though no one notices
our efforts. But there is One who always sees and notices. A
Friend who helps us and sympathizes with us.

Hebrews 4:15 (NIV) says, "We do not have a high priest who
is unable to empathize with our weaknesses, but we have one
who has been tempted in every way, just as we are—yet he did
not sin." Jesus suffered when He was tempted; thus, He is able
to strengthen you when you are tempted (Hebrews 2:18). He said
this: "Watch and pray that you may not enter into temptation.
The spirit indeed is willing, but the flesh is weak" (Matthew 26:41
ESV). You can trust God to always "provide a way out so that you
can endure it" (1 Corinthians 10:13 NIV).

*Because he himself suffered when he was tempted,
he is able to help those who are being tempted.*
HEBREWS 2:18 NIV

PERSONAL APPLICATION:

Are you in need of encouragement? Pour out your heart to your "Friend" Jesus and ask Him to comfort, strengthen, and sustain you. Read your "guidebook"—God's Word—until it's "well worn," and let it bolster your spirits. Finally, write down one of today's Bible verses and "pin it" to your heart or post it on the fridge. Let it be a reminder of God's love and power in your life.

The Bible tells us to "encourage one another and build each other up" (1 Thessalonians 5:11 NIV). Why not *pen* a word of encouragement to someone this week? Everyone enjoys receiving a note from a friend. As you pray today, ask the Lord to show you someone who needs an unexpected boost. Take Marmee's letter as your example and write that person a special note of encouragement and include a verse. You never know how much she might need it!

PRAYER FOR TODAY:

Dearest Jesus, thank You for reminding me that I need words of encouragement when I'm in times of trial or temptation. I need Your help in those moments when I am put to the test and feel overwhelmed. Please give me Your strength to control my thoughts, words, and actions and resist temptation in this area of my life: [your prayer]. Show me who I can send a note of encouragement to today. In Jesus' name, amen.

God blesses those who patiently endure testing and temptation. Afterward they will receive the crown of life that God has promised to those who love him.

JAMES 1:12 NLT

Day 13

LIVING
EXAMPLES

---

*Be imitators of me,
as I am of Christ.*
1 CORINTHIANS 11:1 ESV

> *A shadow passed over the boy's face*
> *as he watched them, feeling that he*
> *ought to go away because uninvited;*
> *yet lingering because home seemed very*
> *lonely and this quiet party in the woods*
> *most attractive to his restless spirit.*
>
> [CHAPTER 13]

This chapter starts with Laurie "luxuriously swinging to and fro in his hammock one warm September afternoon, wondering what his neighbors were about, but too lazy to go and find out." By its end he shifts from wanting to "break away" to see the world and "please" himself to deciding to stay with his grandfather and do his duty. The reason for his radical change of mind: an afternoon spent in good company—with friends who not only call him out for his lazy ways but also challenge him to think beyond his own desires.

When the March girls set off for an afternoon of their Busy Bee Society, Laurie is in "one of his moods." His day has been "unprofitable and unsatisfactory," and he wishes "he could live it over again." He has spent the day shirking his studies, trying Mr. Brooke's patience "to the utmost," displeasing his grandfather, and frightening the maidservants "half out of their wits." He runs to catch up with the girls and finds them on a hill among a grove of trees.

Laurie finds them on their "Delectable Mountain," working happily and industriously at their chosen tasks, and timidly

67

approaches. He is welcomed—as long as he'll work. They discuss their game of playing *Pilgrim's Progress*, their inspiration for working hard, their desire to go to heaven, and their future dreams. Laurie realizes that his dreams—and his attitude and way of living—are selfish. He recognizes the merit of hard work and makes a firm resolution: "I'll let my castle go, and stay with the dear old gentleman while he needs me, for I am all he has."

The March sisters live in a way that is attractive to Laurie— he wants to join their circle, do what they are doing, take part in their fun, and engage in their work. In the same way, we can live lives that attract people to the way we live and follow Christ. Often our lives have a greater impact on others than we realize. Diligence, honesty, kindness, and goodness go such a long way. When we live like Jesus, we draw people closer to us and to God.

When Jesus walked this earth, people were drawn to His incredible kindness, wisdom, and power. In the case of Zacchaeus, he actually climbed a tree to get a glimpse of Jesus because he had heard so much about Him—he was *that* curious! When Jesus saw him, He called him by name and invited Himself into Zacchaeus's life: "Zacchaeus, hurry and come down, for I must stay at your house today" (Luke 19:5 ESV). Zacchaeus came down and received Jesus "joyfully." The result: Zacchaeus confessed his sins to Jesus and received salvation that day!

"This is to my Father's glory, that you bear much fruit, showing yourselves to be my disciples."
JOHN 15:8 NIV

PERSONAL APPLICATION:

Let's be the kind of Christians who attract others to Jesus! Let's make Jesus irresistible to this broken world, both in word and in deed (Colossians 3:17). As you live your life openly and honestly, people will naturally want to spend time with you. Pray for ways to reach out to the "Laurie" who is lonely—and to the "Zacchaeus" who is curious.

Who inspires you and models Christian values to you best? Who challenges you and helps you grow? Seek out friendships with people who are gracious, transparent, wise, and mature in their faith. You can learn a great deal from living, working, and serving alongside other believers who are a little bit further along.

PRAYER FOR TODAY:

Jesus, thank You for coming into my life and heart! I love You with all that I am and all that I have. Help me live a life that draws people closer to You. Show me the lonely person whom I can invite to be part of my daily life. Point out the Zacchaeus who wants to know more about You. Please help me share my faith with my friends and family members: [specific names]. In Jesus' name, amen.

"Let your light shine before others, so that they may see your good works and give glory to your Father who is in heaven."
MATTHEW 5:16 ESV

Day 14

FLEDGLING DREAMS

———◆———

All hard work brings a profit.
PROVERBS 14:23 NIV

> *Jo's eyes sparkled, for it is always pleasant to be believed in, and a friend's praise is always sweeter than a dozen newspaper puffs.*
>
> [CHAPTER 14]

In this chapter about secrets, Jo turns in two stories to a local newspaper in her first effort at getting published. It opens with Jo "very busy" up in the garret on a "chilly" October day. She scribbles away for several hours "till the last page" and signs her name "with a flourish." As she looks over her manuscript, she exclaims, "There, I've done my best! If this won't suit I shall have to wait till I can do better."

Tying up her manuscript with a "smart red ribbon," she sneaks out of the house and goes to town. It takes her several tries, but she finally walks upstairs to the newspaper office, "looking as if she were going to have all her teeth out." When Laurie finds out what she is doing, he encourages her heartily: "It won't fail. . . . Won't it be fun to see them in print, and shan't we feel proud of our authoress?"

When Jo's story is finally published, her family is "delighted." Meg must see Jo's name in print, Amy likes the "artistic parts," and Beth skips and sings with joy. The whole family of "foolish, affectionate people" make a grand "jubilee" out of the occasion. With such a reception, Jo wraps her head "in the paper" and "bedew[s] her little story" with tears. Becoming "independent" and earning "the praise of those she love[s]" is the "dearest" wish of her heart.

Honing our gifts and talents requires time and effort. And becoming really good at something doesn't just happen overnight. We have to take chances, try and fail, and not give up. But the more we practice in private, in our little "garret" rooms—whether it's at work, school, or in the garage—the more fruit we'll see from our efforts. Our fledgling dreams start to take shape as we work hard to practice and perfect the abilities and interests God has placed within us. The best part is when we begin to share our work and use it to bless others.

When God told Moses to build the tabernacle, He chose Bezalel to lead the team of craftsmen. He said to Moses: "I have filled him with the Spirit of God, with ability and intelligence, with knowledge and all craftsmanship, to devise artistic designs, to work in gold, silver, and bronze, in cutting stones for setting, and in carving wood, to work in every craft" (Exodus 31:3–5 ESV). But how did Bezalel become a master craftsman? He most likely honed his remarkable skills *while* in captivity in Egypt. After years of serving Pharaoh, Bezalel got the chance to use his gifts to serve God in a big way!

Whatever your hand finds to do,
do it with all your might.
ECCLESIASTES 9:10 NASB

PERSONAL APPLICATION:

What do you long to do? Where do you feel called to serve? As you pray today, ask God to speak to you about your fledgling dreams. We all have specific callings on our lives, and there are moments when God prompts us to take action and start the process. Sometimes it can take years for the details to come together, but be assured that God is doing a work in your heart all along the way.

If you know someone who is trying something new—going back to school, starting a ministry, applying for adoption, making a career change, or working on a creative endeavor—make it your goal to be a wonderfully "foolish, affectionate" friend. Delight in forward progress, skip and sing when there's good news, and make a "jubilee" over small triumphs.

PRAYER FOR TODAY:

Lord God, thank You for reminding me of the hopes and dreams You've planted in my heart like a seed. I see how some have sprouted and flourished and others are still waiting in the wings. Please speak to me and show me the call You have on my life. Show me if there is a specific prompting of Your Spirit that I need to obey. Help me discern between my own dreams and Your plans for me. Give me the courage to take a step forward in this area: [your prayer]. In Jesus' name, amen.

---

*"I chose you and appointed you
that you should go and bear fruit."*
JOHN 15:16 ESV

Day 15

CHRIST IN THE CRISIS

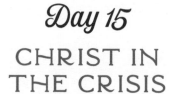

*You will keep in perfect peace
all who trust in you, all whose
thoughts are fixed on you!*
ISAIAH 26:3 NLT

> At the word "telegraph," Mrs. March snatched it, read the two lines it contained, and dropped back into her chair as white as if the little paper had sent a bullet to her heart.
>
> [CHAPTER 15]

In this chapter two short sentences change everything for the March family: "Your husband is very ill. Come at once." The girls gather around their mother, "feeling as if all the happiness and support of their lives was about to be taken from them." Mrs. March says she'll go at once and cries out, "Oh, children, children, help me to bear it!" For several minutes there's "nothing but the sound of sobbing in the room, mingled with broken words of comfort, tender assurances of help, and hopeful whispers that died away in tears."

Hannah recovers and gets to work first, and the rest follow. As Mrs. March organizes the chores, directs the packing, and writes notes, it's all hands on deck. Everyone helps, including Jo, who even cuts and sells her hair—her "one beauty"—to help raise funds. After a harrowing day, they sing tearily through "father's favorite hymn" before bed. The two younger girls fall asleep first "in spite of the great trouble," but the strain of the day keeps the older girls awake. Meg lies "thinking the most serious thoughts she had ever known in her short life," and Jo gives a "stifled sob" over her cropped hair. After a little sisterly talk, they both drop off to sleep.

At midnight Marmee comes through their rooms, "smoothing" their coverlets and "settling" their pillows. She pauses "to look long and tenderly at each unconscious face, to kiss each with lips that mutely blessed, and to pray the fervent prayers which only mothers utter." As she looks out the window at the "dreary night," the moon bursts from behind the clouds like a "bright, benignant, face," and seems to whisper, "Be comforted, dear soul! There is always light behind the clouds."

It's hard to rest during times of distress and anxiety. Our minds and bodies go into overdrive as we run around doing the next thing, feeling harried and overwhelmed. In those moments it's important to remember that Christ is *in* the crisis, right alongside you. When you shift your focus from the chaos in front of you to the strength and power of Jesus *with* you in the trial, something changes. Though it's difficult to believe, even in the midst of turmoil—especially when everything feels out of control—God will give you peace.

It's believed that King David was hiding from his enemies when he wrote Psalm 23, one of the most peaceful and reassuring chapters of the Bible. In it David describes God as a loving shepherd who vigilantly nourishes, guides, and guards His flock. As His sheep, we have everything we need. He leads us to green pastures and beside still waters. He refreshes our souls and directs our paths. Even when we walk through dark valleys, we need not fear any evil, for He is with us. He prepares a table for us in the midst of our enemies. His goodness and love "follow" us all the days of our lives. Above all, He gives us *rest*.

> *"Come to me, all you who are weary*
> *and burdened, and I will give you rest."*
>
> MATTHEW 11:28 NIV

PERSONAL APPLICATION:

When life gets stressful, it's difficult to slow down and focus on the Lord. It's tempting to distract ourselves or stay busy. However, we experience greater peace when we stop to pray and process through everything with God. Make sure you step away from the "fray" today and spend time with Jesus. Picture yourself hand in hand with Him. Give Him all your troubles, for He cares for you (1 Peter 5:7).

It's a rare moment when everything in life is peaceful, so we must create restful habits. Take this time to open your Bible and read Psalm 23 slowly. Put your own name in place of each pronoun to make it personal. Make notes about what you notice, and listen carefully to what God wants to show you. Allow Jesus to lead you beside still waters as you spend time with Him.

PRAYER FOR TODAY:

Thank You, Lord, that You are my good shepherd, my Father, my rock, and my refuge. I want to hide myself in You and enjoy the peace You offer to me. In my daily life, teach me to meditate on Your promises and grow in my ability to trust You. Please help me in the areas of my life where I find it particularly hard to rest my mind and heart. Show me the "light behind the clouds" in this situation: [your prayer]. In Jesus' name, amen.

The peace of God, which surpasses all comprehension, will guard your hearts and minds in Christ Jesus.

PHILIPPIANS 4:7 NASB

Day 16

NEVER FATHERLESS

A father to the fatherless,
a defender of widows,
is God in his holy dwelling.
PSALM 68:5 NIV

> "Hope and keep busy, and whatever happens, remember that you never can be fatherless."
>
> [CHAPTER 16]

In chapter 16 Marmee departs to go nurse Mr. March in Washington. In the early "cold gray dawn," the girls light their lamp and have their morning devotions "with an earnestness never felt before." At breakfast Mrs. March tries to eat but looks "pale and worn with sleeplessness and anxiety." Meg's eyes keep filling, Jo hides her face "more than once," and Beth and Amy each wear a "grave, troubled expression, as if sorrow was a new experience to them."

In the midst of their great trial, there are many small comforts for the March family. Mr. Laurence and Laurie join Hannah in forming a "bodyguard" around the four girls, and "strong and sensible and kind" Mr. Brooke escorts Mrs. March on her journey. Hannah tempts the tearful girls with a "fragrant invitation issuing from the nose of the coffee pot" and helps them exchange their "handkerchiefs for napkins." As Jo and Meg leave for work, Beth remembers "the little household ceremony" and stands in Marmee's place at the window to see them off.

While their mother is away, each girl does her part to "hope and keep busy." They take on new roles and responsibilities, stepping up to the challenge beautifully. With Hannah who is "faithfulness itself" to care for them, Mr. Laurence to "guard" them as if they were "his own," and Laurie to keep them in good spirits, they continue on well. As their father slowly improves, letters fly back and forth to help keep everyone cheerful during their time apart.

The March sisters are surrounded by loving friends in their time of need, but their ultimate Comforter is Jesus—and their first priority is personal devotions. When you're in crisis, make prayer and Bible reading your first line of defense. Ask God for the peace that passes all understanding (Philippians 4:7). Make Him your refuge and your strength (Psalm 46:1). Let Him be your strong tower (Proverbs 18:10). Go to Him first. Go to Him most. Go to Him always.

When King Hezekiah learned that the king of Assyria and his army were coming to destroy Jerusalem, Hezekiah's first response was to go to the temple to pray and ask God for His help and protection (2 Kings 19:14–19). God answered Hezekiah's prayers, declaring that their enemies would not come into the city or even shoot an arrow there: "For I will defend this city to save it, for my own sake and for the sake of my servant David" (2 Kings 19:34 ESV). That night the angel of the Lord went out and struck down the entire enemy camp (2 Kings 19:35).

"I will never leave you nor forsake you."
HEBREWS 13:5 ESV

PERSONAL APPLICATION:

Remember this: You will *never* be fatherless. One of God's most comforting promises is found in Hebrews 13:5 (ESV): "I will never leave you nor forsake you." Memorize it and tuck it away in your heart. Your heavenly Father created you, loves you, and will not abandon you. He is "the Father of mercies and God of all comfort" (2 Corinthians 1:3 ESV). "Draw near to God, and he will draw near to you" (James 4:8 ESV).

We can't help every person in distress, but we can jump in when God calls us to help form the "bodyguard" of love and support during someone's urgent time of need. Get to know your neighbors and check on them regularly. Join the prayer chain or meals ministry at your church. Pray for and touch base with your friends and family members. Most of all, be ready.

———◦•◦———

PRAYER FOR TODAY:

Heavenly Father, thank You that You are always with me, that You will never abandon me or leave me stranded. I need You every day, every hour, every minute. Make me aware of Your holy presence throughout my day today. I want to make it my first response to run to You in good times and bad. Please show me how to provide small comforts for the people in my life who are hurting or in trouble: [your prayer]. In Jesus' name, amen.

*The name of the LORD is a strong tower;
the righteous man runs into it and is safe.*
PROVERBS 18:10 ESV

Day 17
OLD HABITS

*"Stay dressed for action and
keep your lamps burning."*
LUKE 12:35 ESV

> *Relieved of their first anxiety about their father, the girls insensibly relaxed their praiseworthy efforts a little, and began to fall back into old ways.*
>
> [CHAPTER 17]

In this chapter Meg, Jo, and Amy let things slide while Beth bears the weight of burdens that are much too heavy for her to carry. For the first week after Marmee goes away, "the amount of virtue in the old house would have supplied the neighborhood." Everyone seems to be "in a heavenly frame of mind," and self-denial is "all the fashion" in the March home.

However, once they are "relieved" of their "first anxiety about their father," the March sisters relax their "praiseworthy efforts *a little*" (emphasis mine) and begin to "fall back into old ways." As things "grow easier" after such "tremendous exertions," they believe "Endeavor deserve[s] a holiday." Amy lets the housework go, Jo reads books in the garret, and Meg writes letters more than she sews. Meanwhile, Beth continues her own "little duties" faithfully each day, along with those of her sisters, crying and praying in the closet when she's sad or fearful.

It isn't until Beth becomes ill after caring for the Hummel family that everyone wakes up to the reality of what has happened. They all snap to attention and realize the danger of letting things slide: They *had* "done well" and *did* "deserve praise" for their first week's efforts; however, "their mistake was in ceasing to do well." As a result of stopping, they each learn a difficult lesson "through much anxiety and regret."

When a crisis first hits, we usually jump into high gear spiritually. We ramp up our prayer lives, read our Bibles more than usual, and dust off old devotional books. We ask our friends and family for prayer. And we make it a priority to go to church and get the support we need. However, once things start to settle down, we tend to let down our guard "a little" and relax—too much. When we do that, things start to slip through the cracks.

In the Old Testament, the Israelites often let down their guard, fell into old habits, and strayed into sin during times of peace. The lesson for us? We need to be vigilant at all times! In the New Testament, we're instructed to guard our hearts (Proverbs 4:23), devote ourselves to watchful prayer (Colossians 4:2), and be "dressed for action" with our "lamps burning" (Luke 12:35 ESV). First Peter 5:8 (NIV) tells us to be "alert and of sober mind" because our "enemy the devil prowls around like a roaring lion looking for someone to devour." Simply put, our sin nature doesn't take days off; thus, we can never afford a spiritual vacation.

Stay alert! Watch out for your great enemy,
the devil. He prowls around like a roaring lion,
looking for someone to devour.
1 PETER 5:8 NLT

PERSONAL APPLICATION:

Going back to our old fleshly ways is very easy to do. There's no effort in it; it's like coasting downhill. That is why the Bible gives us this important instruction: "Above all else, guard your heart, for everything you do flows from it" (Proverbs 4:23 NIV). When we make it a consistent daily habit to guide our feet down God's paths, guarding our hearts and minds with intention and diligence, it produces steady, long-term fruit in our lives.

When are you most prone to take your foot off the spiritual gas pedal? What tends to happen when you do? It's absolutely necessary to refuel after a great strain, but taking a break from Bible reading, church attendance, or prayer isn't ever part of God's prescription for vibrant spiritual health. Though you can always start fresh, it's harder to get back in gear if you've been coasting. The absolute safest place for you is at Jesus' feet—always.

PRAYER FOR TODAY:

Lord, thank You for this timely reminder that I need to remain spiritually awake. I want to stay close to You and grow steadily in my faith. I don't want to stop and start or become lukewarm. Jesus, please do a new work and spark the fire of personal revival in my heart today. Stir up a renewed passion for Your Word and prayer. Please keep me alert in this area of my life where I tend to let my guard down most often: [your prayer]. In Jesus' name, amen.

---

*Above all else, guard your heart,
for everything you do flows from it.*
PROVERBS 4:23 NIV

Day 18
A LIFELINE

In my distress I called upon the LORD; to my God I cried for help. From his temple he heard my voice, and my cry to him reached his ears.

PSALM 18:6 ESV

> [Jo] could not speak, but she did "hold on," and the warm grasp of the friendly human hand comforted her sore heart, and seemed to lead her nearer to the Divine arm which alone could uphold her in her trouble.
>
> [CHAPTER 18]

When Beth has scarlet fever and Marmee is away, the days feel "dark" and the house seems "sad and lonely." Jo stays by Beth's side, devoting herself to her care "day and night." Beth bears her pain quietly at first, but there comes a time "during the fever fits" that she begins to talk "in a hoarse, broken voice" and "play on the coverlet as if on her beloved little piano." She no longer recognizes the "familiar faces around her" and calls "imploringly for her mother."

Beth's illness affects everyone. Amy is away and lonely with Aunt March, Laurie haunts the house "like a restless ghost," and Mr. Laurence locks up the grand piano because the memories are too painful. Meg and Jo's hearts are "heavy" as they work and wait in the "once happy home." Meg realizes just "how rich she had been in things more precious than any luxuries money could buy—in love, protection, peace, and health, the real blessings of life."

As for Jo, she comes near her breaking point, telling Laurie, "Mother and Father [are] both gone, and God seems so far away I can't find Him." She cries and stretches out her hand "in a helpless sort of way, as if groping in the dark," and Laurie whispers, "I'm here. Hold on to me, Jo, dear!" Jo does "hold on," and the "warm grasp of the friendly human hand comfort[s] her sore heart" and helps "lead her nearer to the Divine arm which alone [can] uphold her in her trouble."

There are times when it feels as though we can't hold on—when God seems "far away" and difficult to find. In our deepest valleys and fiercest trials, we feel helpless, like we're "groping in the dark." There's nothing secure to hold on to, and everything feels shaky. And sometimes, we even lack the strength to reach out to Jesus. It's in those moments—when we can't hold on to God—that He holds on to us.

Psalm 63:8 (ESV) says, "My soul clings to you; your right hand upholds me." As you cling to God, His own powerful right hand holds you and steadies you. Peter knew this firsthand. When he stepped out of the boat to walk on the water to Jesus, he was fine at first. But when he got overwhelmed by the wind and the waves, He quickly began to sink. He cried out to Jesus to save him. And immediately Jesus reached out and took hold of him (Matthew 14:31). If you ever feel like you're sinking, remember that Jesus is right there with you. Cry out to Him and let Him hold you up.

My soul clings to you;
your right hand upholds me.
PSALM 63:8 ESV

PERSONAL APPLICATION:

We all have times when we need someone to hold our hands and steady our hearts. Laurie was there for Jo when she needed a human arm to help "lead her nearer to the Divine arm which alone could uphold her in her trouble." If you're experiencing a deep trial, allow people to come around you with love and support.

If you know someone who is sinking and floundering, reach out your hand and hold on. If a friend is struggling, assure her of God's faithfulness and power. Be the lifeline that reminds others that God is close at hand. It's as simple as saying, "Hold my hand. I'm here for you."

PRAYER FOR TODAY:

Lord Jesus, thank You for this beautiful reminder of Your deep love and care for me. Thank You that You're with me in my darkest hours, holding me and supporting me. Please help me see You and know that You're near each day. I ask You to send me to someone who needs human love and help today. Show me how to strengthen and support these people in their struggles: [specific name(s)]. In Jesus' name, amen.

Encourage one another, especially now that the day of his return is drawing near.
HEBREWS 10:25 NLT

Day 19

SACRED SPACES

———◦•◦———

"But from there you will seek the LORD your God and you will find him, if you search after him with all your heart and with all your soul."

DEUTERONOMY 4:29 ESV

> [Amy] felt the need of some kind hand to hold by so sorely that she instinctively turned to the strong and tender Friend, whose fatherly love most closely surrounds His little children.
>
> [CHAPTER 19]

As Beth's condition worsens, Amy battles against worry for Beth and lonesomeness for her family during her time at Aunt March's house. And though Aunt March does "her best to make Amy happy," she lacks the gift for helping children "feel at home." Instead, she "worries" Amy with her "rules and orders, her prim ways, and long, prosy talks." Amy is troubled by daily chores, tedious books, lectures, and lessons, and Polly, the cranky parrot.

In her "loneliness," Amy aches for support in her faith now that Marmee is far away and Beth is not there to remind her to read her "little book" each morning. When Amy notices that Esther the maid takes "a great deal of comfort" in her private prayers and comes down "looking quiet and satisfied" afterward, Amy asks Esther to help her create a little chapel room where she can "meditate and pray." She fits up a small room with a little table, a footstool in front of it, and a beautiful Bible painting over it.

Amy's little chapel becomes a true place of "solacement" for her "trouble." Amy lays her "little testament and hymnbook" on the table alongside a vase "full of the best flowers" from Laurie.

There she goes each day to sit quietly, think about her family, and pray for Beth. Being "left alone outside the safe home nest," Amy is quite "sincere" in her personal devotions. Her need of "some kind hand to hold by" is so great that she "instinctively turn[s] to the strong and tender Friend, whose fatherly love most closely surrounds His little children."

When we're worried or lonely, the best thing we can do is turn "instinctively" to Jesus, our "strong and tender Friend." It's important to retreat to a quiet place—even for a few moments—and "come away" with Jesus. You can withdraw with God in the middle of a crowded room when needed, but there is something special about stepping away to pray and seek the Lord. Your retreat could be in your bedroom, in your car, in your closet, or on a walk.

Throughout the Bible, God's people turned to Him in times of distress. Moses pleaded with God in the wilderness (Exodus 32:11). Hannah prayed for a child in 1 Samuel (1:10). Hezekiah tore his clothes and went to the temple to pray when faced with an enemy attack (2 Kings 19:1). Queen Esther fasted for three days when her people were threatened (Esther 4:16). And when Peter was in prison, the church earnestly prayed for his release (Acts 12:5). In each case, these men and women discovered that God alone could provide for all their needs when no one else could.

> *But [Jesus] would withdraw*
> *to desolate places and pray.*
> LUKE 5:16 ESV

PERSONAL APPLICATION:

Do you have your own special time and place to meet with Jesus? Take time today to freshen or create your own devotional corner or prayer closet. Set up a little refuge with your Bible, a journal and pen for notes and prayers, and any devotional books or commentaries you like to read. You may also want a cozy blanket and a hot drink on hand. Make a date with Jesus each day and keep it!

Amy missed her mother's spiritual guidance, but "having been taught where to look, she did her best to find the way and walk in it confidingly." If there are younger people in your life or home, help them learn how to have personal devotions. Invite them to join you for your own devotions, and show them how you read your Bible and pray.

PRAYER FOR TODAY:

Thank You, God, that I can retreat with You anytime, anywhere. Teach me to withdraw into that quiet place with You when I'm in the middle of a busy day or a crowded room. Holy Spirit, please stir my heart to pray and seek God throughout the day. I also want to make a special time and place to meet with You daily, Jesus. Help me overcome the obstacles that distract me from my daily devotions: [your prayer]. In Jesus' name, amen.

I meditate on all that you have done;
I ponder the work of your hands.

PSALM 143:5 ESV

Day 20

SEASONS
OF CHANGE

———⋄•⋄———

*"Behold, I am doing a new thing; now it
springs forth, do you not perceive it?"*
ISAIAH 43:19 ESV

> *"Brooke will scratch up a fortune somehow, carry her off, and make a hole in the family, and I shall break my heart, and everything will be abominably uncomfortable."*
>
> [Chapter 20]

In chapter 20 Jo confesses to Marmee that Mr. Brooke has Meg's missing glove. She hopes Marmee will condemn the action, but Marmee's response causes Jo even more anxiety. While Mr. and Mrs. March think Meg is too young for marriage, they've come to admire "John" during their time in Washington. Marmee says he was "so devoted to poor Father that we couldn't help getting fond of him." This makes Jo so unhappy that she gives her hair a "wrathful tweak."

It's not that Jo dislikes Mr. Brooke; it's that she doesn't want to lose Meg. Jo has read enough romance novels to know what's coming: Meg will "go and fall in love," meaning the "end of peace and fun, and cozy times together." Jo is sure that Meg will become "absorbed" with her love life and be "no good" to her anymore. She can't bear the thought of losing Meg and all their happy times: "I just wish I could marry Meg myself, and keep her safe in the family."

Change is never easy. In the brightest seasons of life, we find ourselves wishing we could take a snapshot, hit the Pause button, and linger in the moment. This happens in the "sweet spots" of childhood, parenting, career, ministry, and school. Sometimes we even feel a bit desperate, clinging to precious moments, hoping they'll never end. And especially after a season of heartache, the last thing we want is more change. We just want things to get back to normal!

But remember, our God is a God of new life and resurrection power. He is the God of yesterday, today, *and* tomorrow. He is always on the move, renewing and reshaping us each day. He doesn't often keep us in the same place—or in our comfort zone—for too long. He wants us awake and alert, poised to receive His instructions. While we tend to crave familiarity and ease, God wants us to look to the future with Him and dream big.

The apostle Paul knew a lot about change. Every time the Lord called him into a new territory, it meant leaving behind people he loved. His letters express his deep *longing* to see his Christian brothers and sisters. However, he desired to spread the Gospel even more than he wanted to stay in one place and get comfortable. His life's "ambition" was to "preach the Good News where the name of Christ ha[d] never been heard" (Romans 15:20 NLT). To do that, Paul had to keep pressing forward.

> *"No eye has seen, no ear has heard,*
> *and no mind has imagined what God*
> *has prepared for those who love him."*
>
> 1 CORINTHIANS 2:9 NLT

PERSONAL APPLICATION:

Is there something really good in your life that you wish would stay the same? When faced with change, we sometimes focus on what we'll lose rather than on what we'll gain. If you're in a season of change, ask God to open your eyes to what He has in store for you. While we do need time and space to process big changes, we should also look toward the horizon to see what God wants to do next.

When we're caught up in the goodness of our lives here on earth, we also forget to fix our eyes on eternity with Jesus (Hebrews 12:2). We have a "glorious inheritance" waiting for us in heaven (Ephesians 1:18). And while we're here, we have a mission to fulfill. There are people who need to know Jesus, who need prayer, and who need discipleship. Your life here on earth—in every season—will always be full when it's centered on Jesus.

<hr>

PRAYER FOR TODAY:

Thank You, Jesus, for reminding me that You have good things in store for me here on earth and in heaven. I confess that change is very hard for me. I often grip things too tightly out of fear of losing them. I trust You with my life, Lord, and I ask You now to lead me forward. Open my eyes to the good You're planning. Make me brave and build up my faith. I especially need Your help in this area of change in my life: [your prayer]. In Jesus' name, amen.

"Behold, I am making all things new."
REVELATION 21:5 ESV

Day 21

NEW LEAVES

For it is by grace you have been saved, through faith—and this is not from yourselves, it is the gift of God—not by works, so that no one can boast.
EPHESIANS 2:8–9 NIV

> "I keep turning over new leaves, and spoiling them, as I used to spoil my copybooks, and I make so many beginnings there never will be an end," Laurie said dolefully.
>
> [CHAPTER 21]

In this chapter Laurie gets himself into a terrible scrape and ends up hurting several people he dearly loves. What he means as a silly joke ends up causing a big problem when he writes a letter to Meg as though it's from Mr. Brooke. When Meg answers it, Laurie writes back again. Meg, thinking it's from Mr. Brooke, is horribly embarrassed and finally tells Marmee and Jo.

Even once they realize that Laurie did everything and Mr. Brooke knows nothing about it, it still causes a rift. Marmee has a solemn, private chat with Laurie, after which he is quite changed and penitent. He asks for Meg's forgiveness, which she freely gives, and Jo eventually comes around as well. Unfortunately, Laurie ends up in an even greater row with his grandfather over it, and it falls to Jo to play the part of peacemaker.

When it's time for Laurie to speak to his grandfather, Jo encourages him to "turn over a new leaf and begin again." In a moment of true vulnerability, Laurie confesses that he keeps "turning over new leaves" and "spoiling them," making "so many beginnings there never will be an end" to them. Jo prods him to go eat his dinner and get on with it. As he goes to "partake of humble pie dutifully with his grandfather," Laurie learns an important lesson about grace.

The truth is, we've all been in Laurie's shoes, repeating our mistakes and getting ourselves into scrapes. At times it may feel like you're continually turning over a new leaf. But really that's true for everyone. None of us has done anything to deserve or warrant God's grace. No one gets it right all the time. It's because of Jesus that we're given grace and forgiveness each day: "For from his fullness we have all received, grace upon grace" (John 1:16 ESV). Jesus died on the cross so that we could be set free and made new. Because of the cross there is "therefore now no condemnation for those who are in Christ Jesus" (Romans 8:1 ESV).

The Bible says every person has sinned and fallen short of the glory of God (Romans 3:23). In fact, "there is none righteous, no, not one" (Romans 3:10 KJV). The only One who can wash us clean is Jesus. It is "by grace" that we are saved, "through faith" in Christ, not by good works or perfect behavior (Ephesians 2:8–9 NIV). Our need for God's grace doesn't end the day we get saved. For though the spirit is willing, our flesh is weak and vulnerable (Matthew 26:41). We need more grace every day, every hour, every minute.

> *There is therefore now no condemnation*
> *for those who are in Christ Jesus.*
> ROMANS 8:1 ESV

PERSONAL APPLICATION:

Laurie doesn't see the progress he's making. With each blunder and mistake, he learns a new lesson. And the same is true for you. You *are* growing. New leaves *are* budding. Everyone struggles with something—whether it's a quick temper, fear, pride, control issues, temptations, or unhealthy habits—but it's what we do when we stumble that counts.

When you find yourself repeating old patterns, quickly run to God to repent. When you confess your sins, Jesus is faithful to forgive you and cleanse you of all unrighteousness (1 John 1:9). Go and make things right with anyone you may have hurt. And reach out to a trusted friend or mentor for prayer and guidance. It makes all the difference to have help and support along the way.

———o◆o———

PRAYER FOR TODAY:

Dearest Jesus, thank You for Your grace and mercy and for forgiving me of all my sins. Thank You for picking me up and giving me a fresh start when I falter and stumble. I am desperate for Your grace when I mess up, but I confess that it's hard to give grace to others. I want to turn over a new leaf and make consistent progress. Please work in my life and give me an extra measure of grace in these situations: [your prayer]. In Jesus' name, amen.

If we confess our sins, He is faithful and just to forgive us our sins and to cleanse us from all unrighteousness.

1 JOHN 1:9 NKJV

Day 22

ONE DROP MORE

—◦•◦—

Make us glad for as many days as you have afflicted us, for as many years as we have seen trouble.

PSALM 90:15 NIV

> *Never mind what happened just after that, for the full hearts overflowed, washing away the bitterness of the past and leaving only the sweetness of the present.*
>
> [CHAPTER 22]

In chapter 22 it's Christmas again and the "usual mysteries" of the season "haunt" the March home. Beth grows stronger every day, and Mr. March will "soon be with them." On Christmas Day Beth receives a snow maiden laden with gifts, Amy an engraving, Jo a book, and Meg her first silk dress from Mr. Laurence. But the best is yet to come: "Half an hour after everyone had said they were so happy they could only hold one drop more, the drop came."

Laurie pops his head in at the parlor door and makes a "queer, breathless" announcement: "Here's another Christmas present for the March family." When Mr. March appears, there's "a general stampede" as he becomes "invisible in the embrace of four pairs of loving arms." Beth comes in and runs straight into her father's arms, and in that moment "full hearts" overflow, "washing away the bitterness of the past and leaving only the sweetness of the present."

After a delicious Christmas dinner, the "happy family" sits together around the fire. Jo remembers how they groaned over their "dismal Christmas" the year before. Meg claims it was "a pleasant year on the whole," but Amy says it's been a "pretty hard one" and Beth says she's "glad it's over." Mr. March encourages them with this: "You have got on bravely, and I think the burdens are in a fair way to tumble off very soon."

When you're in the middle of a long trial, it sometimes seems like the sun will never shine again. You focus on getting through each day, unable to see the way ahead, doing the best you can with what you have. But, oh, what a sweet relief it is to come to the end of a long trial. There's an overwhelming sense of thankfulness. It's as though the sun has peeked out from behind the clouds and you can breathe again.

Be encouraged! A day is coming when all of our burdens will tumble off and everything will be made new in Christ. On that day, when we finally see Jesus face-to-face, we will run into His arms and never let go. He will wipe away every tear; there will be no more death, crying, or pain (Revelation 21:4). We won't be able to hold "one drop more" as our "full hearts" overflow with joy. His presence and fullness will wash away "the bitterness of the past," and "only the sweetness" of forever with Him will remain.

*"He will wipe away every tear from their eyes,
and death shall be no more, neither shall there
be mourning, nor crying, nor pain anymore,
for the former things have passed away."*
REVELATION 21:4 ESV

PERSONAL APPLICATION:

The March family is surrounded by good friends and neighbors through all their ups and downs. May this chapter inspire you to gather and connect with family and friends this week. Make it a priority to meet together regularly with other Christians for Bible study, fellowship, food, and prayer (Acts 2:42; Hebrews 10:25). Join hands, support one another, laugh and cry across the table together, and create deep, lasting bonds.

Are you in the midst of a great trial? Are you longing for relief? It's often hard to believe things will get better when you're knee-deep in pain, sorrow, or strain. Remember this: Jesus can and will calm the wind and the waves of your storm (Mark 4:39). Nothing is impossible for God. There *will* be a day when your heart is full again.

PRAYER FOR TODAY:

Lord Jesus, You are always faithful in every season and in every trial. Thank You for the promise of heaven and eternity spent with You. Please help me build stronger bonds with my brothers and sisters in Christ. Show me where to invest in deeper relationships and who to spend time with around the table this week. I especially ask for strength and relief in this trying area of my life: [your prayer]. In Jesus' name, amen.

"I will restore to you the years that the swarming locust has eaten."
JOEL 2:25 ESV

Day 23

LOVE WORTH FIGHTING FOR

⊰⊷◆⊶⊱

I count everything as loss because of the surpassing worth of knowing Christ Jesus my Lord.

<small>PHILIPPIANS 3:8 ESV</small>

> "I'm not afraid of being poor,
> for I've been happy so far,
> and I know I shall be with
> him because he loves me."
>
> [CHAPTER 23]

In this chapter Meg faces a decision that changes the course of her life. And it isn't just about her feelings for Mr. Brooke or whether she wants to marry him. Rather, it's about how she'll live her life and what's most important to her. Will she live for herself and make material wealth the focus of her life, or will she marry the good, loving man standing in front of her even if it means being poor? Does she want a life of luxury or a life of love?

With so much at stake, Meg meets with plenty of temptation. She fluctuates between sending John off with a quick refusal to softening at the sight of "so much love" in his eyes. When he grows confident, she gives in to her own vanity and toys with his emotions. But when Aunt March arrives, Meg finds out her true feelings. She realizes in that moment—as she defends Mr. Brooke—that she does love John despite his "poverty."

In this scene, Meg makes a proclamation about her life. She decides Marmee was right when she said, "I'd rather see you poor men's wives, if you were happy, beloved, contented, than queens on thrones, without self-respect and peace" (ch. 9). Meg realizes that she's "not afraid of being poor" because she has "been happy so far" in her life despite not being rich (ch. 23). She wants a home filled with harmony and happiness more than she wants fancy dresses, houses, or finery.

There are many such defining moments in life—when we decide what's most important to us. And the same is true in our spiritual lives. Each of us has a moment when we must choose who we will serve: Jesus or anything/anybody else. And there are a multitude of other everyday moments afterward when we must live it out. But the more we follow Him, the more we experience the truth of Paul's incredible statement: "Indeed, I count everything as loss because of the surpassing worth of knowing Christ Jesus my Lord" (Philippians 3:8 ESV).

After her husband died, Ruth faced a life-altering decision (Ruth 1). She could go back to her parents' home and their gods or move to a new country with her mother-in-law, Naomi, and follow her God. Ruth could stay where she was safe, comfortable, and known, or she could walk with Naomi into the unknown—to a place where she would be a foreigner without a family, a job, or a home. In a truly defining moment, Ruth decided to leave her old life behind and follow the one, true God. She counted all things a loss for the sake of knowing and following God.

"Your hearts therefore shall be wholly devoted to the LORD our God."

1 KINGS 8:61 NASB

PERSONAL APPLICATION:

Truly, there is nothing in this world that is worth more than knowing and following Jesus. With Him we are "happy, beloved, contented." Through faith in Him, we have become His coheirs (Roman 8:17) that we might receive incomparable and lasting riches that will never spoil or fade (1 Peter 1:4). When we walk through life with Jesus, there is joy unspeakable. Nothing else compares to knowing Him.

Are you at a crossroads moment in your faith? Jesus is standing in front of you, offering you His love, new life, and eternity spent with Him. If there is anything keeping you from pursuing a deep, personal walk with Him, take this time to pray and bring it all to Him now. Living a life devoted to loving and serving Jesus is truly the best life you could ever live.

PRAYER FOR TODAY:

Lord Jesus, thank You for loving me, thank You for forgiving me, thank You for saving me. I choose to follow You today, tomorrow, and every day. I want eternal riches over earthly splendor. I want a life and home filled with love. I confess my desire for comfort, finery, and the pleasures of life. Please focus my attention on what truly matters. Help me take a stand for my faith in the areas where I am most shaky: [your prayer]. In Jesus' name, amen.

"Choose this day whom you will serve. . . . But as for me and my house, we will serve the LORD."

JOSHUA 24:15 ESV

Day 24

WONDERFUL COUNSELORS

❧━◆━❧

If you need wisdom, ask our generous God, and he will give it to you. He will not rebuke you for asking.
JAMES 1:5 NLT

Three years have now passed for our beloved March family. John is back from the war and working as a bookkeeper as he and Meg prepare for their wedding. Marmee, Hannah, and the girls have helped Meg set up housekeeping in the "Dovecote." Laurie has finished college, and Jo continues to write. Beth is stronger now but still in "delicate" health, while Amy has blossomed into a pretty young woman with many admirers.

The March sisters are blessed with two godly parents, and in this chapter we learn more about Mr. March, "the quiet scholar, sitting among his books. . .the head of the family, the household conscience, anchor, and comforter." As the pastor of a small parish, Mr. March is described as "a minister by nature as by grace, a quiet, studious man, rich in the wisdom that is better than learning, the charity which calls all mankind 'brother,' the piety that blossoms into character, making it august and lovely."

This loving, studious, and charitable minister knows no "worldly successes," and yet "as naturally as sweet herbs draw bees," people are drawn to Mr. March. Earnest young men find him "young at heart," while "thoughtful or troubled" women are "sure of finding the gentlest sympathy, the wisest counsel." Sinners are "rebuked and saved," "gifted" men enjoy his companionship, and ambitious men catch "glimpses of nobler ambitions than their own." Even unbelievers come to him, admitting that his beliefs are "beautiful and true."

We all need wise mothers and fathers, counselors, mentors, and teachers. We can learn so much from those who have marked out a life committed to following Jesus Christ. They can provide sympathy, wise counsel, exhortation, correction, and companionship. We need glimpses of "nobler ambitions" than our own—people who show the way, point us in the right direction, change our perspective, and steady our stumbling feet.

Stepping into Mr. March's study must have been comforting, warm, and inviting. The same is true when we step into the counsel halls of God's Word. When we meet with Jesus, He provides the sympathy, help, and guidance we need. Isaiah 9:6 (NIV) describes Him as our "Wonderful Counselor, Mighty God, Everlasting Father, Prince of Peace." He is our High Priest who is *able* to "empathize with our weaknesses" (Hebrews 4:15 NIV). He doesn't look down on us or shame us. And He gives wisdom *liberally* without judgment when we ask (James 1:5).

Let us then with confidence draw near
to the throne of grace, that we may receive
mercy and find grace to help in time of need.
HEBREWS 4:16 ESV

PERSONAL APPLICATION:

Do you need a loving Father? A comforter? A compassionate counselor? Jesus promises to be all of those things and more for you. And He has sent the Holy Spirit to be your helper (John 14:26). As you spend time with Jesus today, picture yourself coming in and sitting down with Him in a quiet study. Bring Him all that's on your heart today, and ask for His comfort and guidance.

If you're longing for earthly counselors, father and mother figures, and loving comforters in your life, ask God to bring godly people into your life who can take up those positions. Find a church with solid teaching and loving, studious, and charitable leaders. Join a Bible study with people who are serious about their faith. Start today by asking God to connect you with *one* godly mentor. Pray every day and watch what God will do.

———◦◆◦———

PRAYER FOR TODAY:

Lord Jesus, thank You for being my Wonderful Counselor,
my Mighty God, my Everlasting Father, my Prince of Peace.
I want to walk on Your paths of righteousness for Your name's
sake (Psalm 23:3). Please guide me as I read Your Word and
pray. Speak clearly to me through Your Holy Spirit. I ask
especially for wise mentors to guide me. Please counsel me
in this area of my life: [your prayer]. In Jesus' name, amen.

Listen to advice and accept instruction,
that you may gain wisdom in the future.
PROVERBS 19:20 ESV

Day 25

ADORNED
WITH LOVE

———◦•◦———

*See what great love the Father has lavished on us,
that we should be called children of God!*

1 JOHN 3:1 NIV

> "That is the prettiest wedding I've been to for an age, Ned, and I don't see why, for there wasn't a bit of style about it," observed Mrs. Moffat to her husband.
>
> [CHAPTER 25]

Despite her adolescent dreams of a rich and elegant life, Meg plans a wedding that is simple and sweet: "I don't want a fashionable wedding, but only those about me whom I love, and to them I wish to look and be my familiar self." On her wedding day, she looks like a rose, "for all that was best and sweetest in heart and soul seemed to bloom into her face that day, making it fair and tender, with a charm more beautiful than beauty."

Meg decides to forgo silk, lace, and orange flowers; instead, she makes her own wedding gown, "sewing into it the tender hopes and innocent romances of a girlish heart." She has her hair "braided up" by her sisters and carries lilies of the valley, John's favorite. She tells her sisters to hug her close and put as many "crumples" in her dress as possible. Before the ceremony, Meg ties John's cravat and spends "a few minutes with Father quietly in the study."

At the quaint reception, there is no "display of gifts" or "elaborate breakfast." Rather, everyone enjoys a "plentiful lunch of cake and fruit, dressed with flowers." They walk together in twos and threes, enjoying the sunshine, and Laurie arranges a festive, impromptu dance. When Meg later makes "the quiet walk with John from the old home to the new," she goes "with her hands full of flowers and the June sunshine brightening her happy face."

Meg is adorned with the most precious thing of all—love. And the same is true for you as a beloved son or daughter of the King. First John 3:1 (NIV) says, "What great love the Father has lavished on us, that we should be called children of God!" Through faith in Jesus, you are a child of God forever (Galatians 3:26). God has "dressed" you in the "clothing of salvation" and "draped" you in a "robe of righteousness" (Isaiah 61:10 NLT). And as you reflect His glory, you are being transformed into the image of Christ with each passing day (2 Corinthians 3:18).

In the New Testament, wedding imagery is used to describe our new identity in Christ. Jesus is referred to as the Bridegroom and the Church as His bride. Revelation 19:7 (NASB) describes this heavenly scene: "Let's rejoice and be glad and give the glory to Him, because the marriage of the Lamb has come, and His bride has prepared herself." One day we'll wear "fine linen, bright and pure" (Revelation 19:8 ESV) and eat with Jesus at the wedding supper of the Lamb (Revelation 19:9). On that glorious day, we'll be united with Him forever!

I am overwhelmed with joy in the LORD my God!
For he has dressed me with the clothing of salvation
and draped me in a robe of righteousness.
ISAIAH 61:10 NLT

PERSONAL APPLICATION:

Is there something in your life that isn't quite what you imagined it would be? Meg's wedding day reminds us that many of life's sweetest moments have nothing to do with frills or fanfare but about the people gathered and the love expressed. As you pray today, ask God to adorn your life and your plans with His love. He will help you look past your material concerns and find exquisite beauty at the center of it all.

Sally Moffat noticed that something was different about Meg's wedding, even though it wasn't stylish. You may feel as though you live a simple life that isn't fashionable or fancy, but people notice that your life is different—in a good way. As you live and serve God quietly, without fanfare, pray for ways to lavish His love on your friends and neighbors. The way you live helps others see that a life of faith is very beautiful indeed.

PRAYER FOR TODAY:

Lord God, thank You for Your abundant love. I see Your special touches all over my life. I confess I sometimes get too focused on what I want rather than all You've given me. Please prepare me so that I can bloom in every season. I want to be remade into Your image, Jesus. I especially need Your love to adorn this area of my life: [your prayer]. In Jesus' name, amen.

But we all, with unveiled faces, looking as in a mirror at the glory of the Lord, are being transformed into the same image from glory to glory, just as from the Lord, the Spirit.

2 Corinthians 3:18 nasb

Day 26

FRUITFUL
FAILURES

*And endurance develops
strength of character.*
ROMANS 5:4 NLT

> [Amy] persevered in spite of all obstacles, failures, and discouragements, firmly believing that in time she should do something worthy.
>
> [CHAPTER 26]

In this chapter Amy shows a growing interest in the arts and in being "an attractive and accomplished woman." The opening pages catalog her attempts at "every branch of art." She experiments with pen-and-ink drawings, oil paintings, charcoal portraits, clay sculpting, plaster molding, sketches from nature, and even hot "poker-sketching" on pieces of wood. Though none of her artistic endeavors turn into masterpieces, she throws herself into each project with wholehearted zeal.

Amy then decides to entertain her high society friends with a day's outing and lunch. She plans the menu, the recreation, the invitations, and even the budget. Though everyone thinks she should keep things simple and tasteful rather than try to meet standards she can't possibly meet, she sticks to her plan with determination. Nothing comes together like she hopes, and her attempts end badly despite her best efforts. She thanks her family for helping and asks them not to "allude to it for a month, at least!"

On the surface, this chapter seems like a laundry list of Amy's failures, but it actually tells us a lot about Amy's undaunted efforts to try, try, and try again. No, she doesn't get things right at first. No, she doesn't always have her priorities in place. But as she goes, she keeps learning. She doesn't let disasters, injuries, or even the laughter of others keep her from pressing on to reach her goals. Amy perseveres "in spite of all obstacles, failures, and discouragements."

We can learn much from Amy's refusal to give up "in spite" of all her failed experiments. We often think that perfection is the main objective, but it's what happens during our climb that matters most. There's growth that happens *while* we're faltering, slipping, and sliding that can't be manufactured in any other way. When we persevere despite ninety-nine failures—even when everyone around us has moved on, given up, or laughed it off—that's when God molds and shapes us into His vessels.

Have you ever wondered how David was able to knock out Goliath with just a slingshot and one stone? Yes, David's faith played a huge role in his success, and, yes, God was with him in a miraculous way. But it also wasn't David's first time slinging stones. He'd spent hours, days, months, and years with a slingshot and a handful of stones in the fields where he helped guard his father's sheep. He'd killed many wild animals to protect the sheep, but there were likely a lot of missed shots along the way. When he faced off against Goliath, David's precision came from years of trying—and failing—until he eventually learned to hit his mark every single time.

He chose David his servant and
took him from the sheepfolds.
PSALM 78:70 ESV

PERSONAL APPLICATION:

God loves every attempt you make to follow Him, persevere in your faith, and develop your spiritual gifts and natural talents to serve and glorify Him. He delights in your undaunted pursuit of a holy life, holy dreams, and holy aspirations. He sees every gift He placed within your mind and body, and He loves to see you activate those gifts in practical ways!

All great endeavors start with many fruitful failures. Don't give up on your most tender dreams. Don't ignore that thing you really love to do. Persevere despite all obstacles, failures, and discouragements. Ask God to take your hopes (and doubts) and show you how you can best serve Him and love others with everything that's within you. Your first, second, or hundredth attempt might not be perfect, but God will mold and shape your efforts. Keep seeking Him, keep working as unto the Lord, and keep dedicating yourself to Him. And while you're at it, make sure you encourage the people around you to do the same.

PRAYER FOR TODAY:

Dear Jesus, sometimes I feel like I'm bubbling up with all the things I feel called to do, and sometimes I get discouraged and lose steam. Please stir me up and get me moving. Redirect my path if I'm not quite where You want me to go yet. Help me hear Your voice and obey it. I dedicate all that's within me to You, and I ask Your special blessing on my efforts in this area of my life: [your prayer]. In Jesus' name, amen.

Commit your work to the Lord,
and your plans will be established.
PROVERBS 16:3 ESV

Day 27

GROCERIES
AND GOWNS

*Each of you should use whatever gift
you have received to serve others.*
1 PETER 4:10 NIV

> To the seaside they went, after much discussion, and though Beth didn't come home as plump and rosy as could be desired, she was much better, while Mrs. March declared she felt ten years younger.
>
> [CHAPTER 27]

Every few weeks Jo shuts herself "up in her room," puts on her "scribbling suit," and falls into a "vortex" of writing. She wears a "black woolen pinafore" and "a cap of the same material, adorned with a cheerful red bow." The cap acts as a "beacon," allowing her family to gauge her mood depending on how it's worn. When a "writing fit" comes on, Jo goes completely into her own world, living without much sleep or food.

But when Jo begins to earn an income with her stories, her writing goals shift. She no longer thinks solely about fame, fortune, or grand adventures; instead, she wants to help her family. With her first check, she sends Beth and Mrs. March to the seaside. When they return refreshed, Jo falls to work "with a cheery spirit, bent on earning more of those delightful checks." Her stories provide for the butcher's bill, a new carpet, and "groceries and gowns."

Jo is learning to use her gifts to serve others. As the tender and fiercely protective side of her personality activates, Jo realizes she can use her writing to help her family. Yes, she has higher ideals for her writing. Yes, she still has important lessons to learn. But this chapter shows a shift in Jo's personal goals: While she hopes to write something truly good and worthwhile one day, she wants to care for the people she loves even more than she wants to be a famous author.

We each have a great call on our lives to work with purpose and excellence, producing fruit that will last and make a difference in the world. There are seasons when God opens up the time, space, and opportunity to spread our wings and focus on the goals and purposes He has placed in our hearts. And there are other seasons when God asks us to love and care for others first. When we begin to use our gifts and talents for the good of another, we find great spiritual treasure.

Lydia was one of the first converts on Paul's missionary journey to Philippi (Acts 16 NIV). They met on the Sabbath "outside the city gate" at a "place of prayer" by the river. As a "dealer in purple cloth," Lydia was wealthy and successful. When she heard Paul's message, "the Lord opened her heart to respond." She and her household were baptized, and she invited Paul and his companions to her house. Later she generously opened her home as a meeting place for "the brothers and sisters"—the first "church" in her city!

> *God is not unjust; he will not forget your work and the love you have shown him as you have helped his people and continue to help them.*
> HEBREWS 6:10 NIV

PERSONAL APPLICATION:

Is God calling you to use your gifts to help others? Your time and know-how are of great worth. No matter your "day" job—whether you're a fund-raiser, a student, a stay-at-home parent, a coach, a construction worker, a retired teacher, an IT director, or a banker—you can use your skill set to provide help, advice, and services for others in God's family. God has given you specific gifts for a purpose.

Jo types often have the energy and capacity to take on extra work and shoulder large burdens. They're steady, sturdy, and reliable. However, because they're so "others-focused," they often put their own needs last. If you know a Jo, help her make time for something she loves to do. (It might be a project!) If you *are* a Jo, don't be afraid to let others share their talents with you and use the gifts the Lord has given them.

PRAYER FOR TODAY:

Lord God, thank You for the jobs You've given me to do.
I offer up my work, my abilities, and my experiences to You.
Show me if there's a need I can meet out of my resources,
something I can do to help, a small comfort I can provide,
or a gift I can give. Enlarge my faith so I might give freely
and lovingly. Please make me generous with this part of my
life and work: [your prayer]. In Jesus' name, amen.

Therefore, as we have opportunity, let us do good to all,
especially to those who are of the household of faith.
GALATIANS 6:10 NKJV

Day 28

JELLY STAINS AND
GROWING PAINS

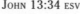

*"A new commandment I give to you,
that you love one another: just as I have
loved you, you also are to love one another."*
JOHN 13:34 ESV

> *Meg learned to love her husband better for his poverty, because it seemed to have made a man of him, given him the strength and courage to fight his own way, and taught him a tender patience.*
>
> [CHAPTER 28]

In this chapter we follow John and Meg inside the "Dovecote" as they traverse their first year of marriage. They soon find out that even the most gentle and well-meaning people undergo times of relational difficulty and discord. As they walk through several rocky patches, they learn how to love each other more—and love themselves less—ending the year with the arrival of their darling twin babies, Daisy and Demi.

When John brings home a friend for dinner unannounced on the very day Meg tries to make jelly for the first time, everything goes downhill fast. John is embarrassed and disappointed to find a tearful, jelly-stained wife and no food on the table. Meg is exhausted and upset that John brought home a surprise guest on exactly the wrong day. John becomes angry, and Meg goes to bed in tears. That evening they learn their first lesson in apologies and soft hearts.

Later, when Meg uses the money for John's new coat to buy material for a silk dress for herself, she says she's "tired of being poor." He responds kindly but is deeply hurt. Meg, heartbroken and remorseful, sells the fabric to buy his new coat. In a tender moment of reconciliation, their relationship is restored and even strengthened as they each continue to practice the intricate art of loving one another better than themselves.

This chapter showcases the simple fact that relationships—even with the people we love most—aren't easy. They take work, patience, humility, forgiveness, and strength of character. Love isn't a light switch we can turn on and keep on; it's a daily choice to put the other person first and choose to speak, act, and listen in a biblical way despite how we might feel.

First Corinthians 13:4–7 (NIV) defines love like this: "Love is patient, love is kind. It does not envy, it does not boast, it is not proud. It does not dishonor others, it is not self-seeking, it is not easily angered, it keeps no record of wrongs. Love does not delight in evil but rejoices with the truth. It always protects, always trusts, always hopes, always perseveres." In other words, true love—God's kind of love—goes against all of our human desires and tendencies. It means we care about people more than we care about being right or getting what we want.

Do nothing out of selfish ambition or vain conceit.
Rather, in humility value others above yourselves.

PHILIPPIANS 2:3 NIV

PERSONAL APPLICATION:

We cannot love people out of thin air. Love has a source, and that source is God (1 John 4:7). Without Him we can try really hard, but even with the best intentions, we'll come up short every time. Come before Jesus now, and lay down all your relationship frustrations and hurt feelings at His feet. Ask Him to fill you with His patience and love for the people in your life.

All relationships experience growing pains and difficult days. It's important that we remember who the real enemy is. When you're angry, hurt, or in an argument, your true enemy is *not* the person standing in front of you. A spiritual battle is going on as well. If you're facing strife, make prayer your first defense. Go to Jesus and ask Him to calm any spiritual attacks, equip you with the full armor of God (Ephesians 6), and place a hedge of protection around you and your relationships (Job 1:10).

PRAYER FOR TODAY:

Thank You, Jesus, for this beautiful example of how to grow closer to the people I love. I ask You now to fill me to overflowing with Your compassion, kindness, and forgiveness in my own personal relationships. Please give me a humble heart and help me put others before myself. Show me where I'm being self-centered. I especially need Your love and grace to overflow in this relationship: [your prayer]. In Jesus' name, amen.

Search for peace, and work to maintain it.
PSALM 34:14 NLT

Day 29

CARELESS
WORDS

———◦•◦———

Set a guard, O Lord, over my mouth;
keep watch over the door of my lips!

PSALM 141:3 ESV

> By her next speech, Jo deprived
> herself of several years of pleasure,
> and received a timely lesson in the
> art of holding her tongue.
>
> [CHAPTER 29]

When Jo agrees to dress up and go along with Amy on morning calls, she decides to make a game of it and take Amy's advice before each visit quite literally. At the first home, she is "calm, cool, and quiet," playing the part of a "prim young lady." When they leave, the ladies of the house call her a "haughty, uninteresting creature." At the next house, she promises to be "a charming girl" and "gossip and giggle, and have horrors and raptures." This time "nothing could have been worse" than Jo's embarrassing behavior and "awful" stories.

At the third home, Amy gives up trying. Jo acts like her old self and ends up soiling her dress, gloves, and bonnet while playing with the boys of the house and their dog. From there they go to Aunt March's house, with Amy's clothing still "fresh and spotless" and Jo's "damaged costume" rumpled and dirty and her bonnet full of crumbs. However, it's not Jo's appearance that spoils the day and deprives her of "several years of pleasure"; it's her attitude and words.

While Amy talks politely with her aunts, Jo speaks brusquely about getting help from others, saying, "I don't like favors, they oppress and make me feel like a slave. I'd rather do everything for myself, and be perfectly independent." When asked about her French, she says she doesn't "know a word" and "can't bear French" because it's "such a slippery, silly sort of language." Little does Jo know, but her words help make the final decision regarding which March sister will get to go to Europe.

Jo's careless speech, and the pain and consequences that come with it, can teach us a "timely lesson" in the art of holding our tongues. There are many moments in life when we look back and wish we'd kept our mouths closed, either because we said something we shouldn't, said more than we wanted to, or even said something that wasn't truly what we meant or felt. The tongue is powerful, and we need to guard it well.

James writes about the power of the tongue and how difficult the tongue is to tame, likening it to a fire: "So also the tongue is a small member, yet it boasts of great things. How great a forest is set ablaze by such a small fire!" (James 3:5 ESV). He says "no human being can tame the tongue" because it's "a restless evil, full of deadly poison" (v. 8 ESV). With it people can "bless our Lord and Father" and "curse people who are made in the likeness of God" (v. 9 ESV). Though it's small, the tongue can do a lot of damage or a lot of good.

From the same mouth come
blessing and cursing.
JAMES 3:10 ESV

PERSONAL APPLICATION:

If you tend to say things you later regret, ask the Holy Spirit to help you know when to zip your lip, and stop to pray before you speak. What we say ultimately flows from what is hidden in our hearts (Luke 6:45), so make it a regular habit to ask God to search your heart and cleanse you of all ill will, anger, jealousy, frustration, and pride.

Here's the good news: While our tongues can be a curse, they can also be a blessing! Let's make it our aim to use our tongues for good—to build people up instead of tear them down. We can encourage one another and lift each other's spirits (1 Thessalonians 5:11). We can pray, share Bible stories and personal testimonies, and sing spiritual songs and hymns (Ephesians 5:19). And we can share the Gospel with people who have never heard it before.

PRAYER FOR TODAY:

Thank You, Lord, for this timely reminder about the power of my tongue. Please teach me to use my words not to tear down or complain but to build up and edify. Search my heart, O God, and show me where I need to confess any bitterness, anger, or frustration. Please set a guard over my heart and my mouth. May my speech be pleasing in Your sight. I ask now for Your help to watch my tongue in these situations and with these people: [your specific request]. In Jesus' name, amen.

---

*Let everything you say be good and helpful,
so that your words will be an encouragement
to those who hear them.*

EPHESIANS 4:29 NLT

Day 30

TAKE THE HIGH ROAD

*When he was reviled, he did not revile in return;
when he suffered, he did not threaten, but continued
entrusting himself to him who judges justly.*
1 PETER 2:23 ESV

> *Amy's conscience preached her a little sermon from that text, then and there, and she did what many of us do not always do, took the sermon to heart, and straightway put it in practice.*
>
> [CHAPTER 30]

Mrs. Chester's fair is so "elegant" and "select" that it is considered a "great honor by the young ladies of the neighborhood to be invited to take a table." However, when Mrs. Chester moves Amy to the little girls' flower table due to gossip about the March girls and jealousy on her daughter May's part, it's a terrible snub. Even though Amy has already set up the art table and her own art so beautifully, she kindly moves to the flower table despite hurt feelings.

At home everyone feels "great indignation" about Amy's treatment, but Amy insists on carrying out her task with politeness and poise: "Because they are mean is no reason why I should be. I hate such things, and though I think I've a right to be hurt, I don't intend to show it." Amy sticks to her "resolution" in spite of "various very natural temptations to resent and retaliate." She turns the other cheek and acts with complete kindness throughout the fair.

At the height of the crisis, Amy finds a Bible verse pasted in a scrapbook she has been making. It provides "a silent reminder" that helps carry her through: "Thou shalt love thy neighbour as thyself" (Matthew 22:39 KJV). This and other verses provide a "sweet rebuke" for all the "heartburnings and uncharitableness of spirit" she feels. Amy takes the "sermon to heart, and straightway put[s] it in practice," living out her faith by behaving beautifully and finishing well.

It's true that many "wise and true sermons are preached us every day by unconscious ministers in street, school, office, or home." God can use any situation as a "pulpit." In the face of frustration and injustice, we can fight, make a speech, and throw a fit, or we can choose to simmer down, say a prayer, and walk forward with grace and humility. Things won't always turn out perfectly every time, but when you follow God's ways, you can be assured that He will make it right in the end.

In Genesis 39 Joseph was sent to prison for a crime he didn't commit. But his story isn't a record of his bitterness, his stubborn refusal to cooperate, or his personal fight for freedom and justice. Instead, his story is about how he received God's blessing there in the prison: "But the LORD was with Joseph and extended kindness to him, and gave him favor in the sight of the warden of the prison" (Genesis 39:21 NASB). Joseph trusted God to defend him, make things right, and ultimately set him free. Later God used Joseph in a mighty way!

> *"Love your enemies, do good to those*
> *who hate you, bless those who curse you,*
> *and pray for those who spitefully use you."*
> LUKE 6:27–28 NKJV

PERSONAL APPLICATION:

What do you do when you're faced with personal insults or injustices? Your words, actions, and responses speak volumes about your character. When you conduct yourself well in times of stress, accusations, unfair treatment and unkindness, it is a living testimony to your faith in Christ. When you "turn the other cheek" (Matthew 5:39), your actions bring honor to His name.

Certain circumstances and relationships require an extra measure of restraint to remain calm and keep a quiet spirit. And nobody gets it right every time. But with time, prayer, and practice, you *will* make progress. And be assured that Jesus is right by your side. You don't have to defend yourself; the Lord will defend you and keep you and carry you.

PRAYER FOR TODAY:

Lord Jesus, I confess that I struggle to turn the other cheek and love my neighbor when people hurt me or the people I love. My first response is to defend myself, fight back, or tell others what happened. Teach me to live out my faith in humility and grace. May my life, my words, and my actions be pleasing to You, O Lord. Please be my strong defender in this difficult situation: [your prayer]. In Jesus' name, amen.

Let the words of my mouth and the meditation of my heart be acceptable in Your sight, O LORD, my strength and my Redeemer.
PSALM 19:14 NKJV

141

Day 31

GUIDING
LIGHTS

*Where there is no guidance, a people falls,
but in an abundance of counselors there is safety.*

PROVERBS 11:14 ESV

> *"Send me as much advice as you like;*
> *I'll use it if I can. I wish I could see*
> *you for a good talk, Marmee."*
> [CHAPTER 31]

Amy's first venture out into the world without her parents or sisters is a wonderful and exhilarating experience. She sees the beautiful sights of England, France, and Germany, all while traveling in style with her aunt and uncle. In England she says she feels "like a dissipated London fine lady, writing here so late, with my room full of pretty things, and my head a jumble of parks, theaters, new gowns, and gallant creatures."

When she realizes Fred Vaughn might propose, Amy writes to tell Marmee that she has decided to say, "Yes, thank you." Her reasons are simple: he's "handsome, young, clever enough, and very rich." However, though it seems like she has made up her mind, Amy ends her letter by asking Marmee to "send as much advice" as she likes, saying she wishes she could see her for a "good talk." As she invites her mother to give her the guidance she needs, we see an older, wiser Amy emerge.

Amy is a different person now than the little girl who burned Jo's manuscript, took pickled limes to school, and made up her own last will and testament. She has learned to pray, read her Bible, work hard, and turn the other cheek. She has made it her goal to "be what Mother is." She wants to be "a true gentle-woman in mind and manners" who is "above the little mean-nesses and follies and faults that spoil so many women" (ch. 30). Best of all, she's open to wise counsel.

It's a mark of maturity to ask for input from others. The act of opening ourselves up to hearing from our friends, family members, and mentors is an act of humility—especially when we know they might not say what we want to hear. But when we seek wise counsel and take it to heart, we give the Lord an opportunity to speak into our lives in a broader way. Whether we get the confirmation we want or we're advised to put on the brakes, getting godly advice is always best. As the Bible says, we easily fall when we don't ask for guidance, but there is "safety" in a "multitude of counselors" (Proverbs 11:14 NKJV).

The Bible provides many examples of people who profited from the wisdom and experience of others. Moses' father-in-law advised him to appoint men to help oversee the Israelites and judge their daily disputes (Exodus 18). Mordecai provided Queen Esther with insight, instruction, and courage when she needed to speak up on behalf of her people (Esther 4). And when Barnabas and Saul were faced with the question of circumcision for Gentile believers, they sought the counsel of the apostles and elders in Jerusalem (Acts 15).

Listen to advice and accept discipline, and at the end you will be counted among the wise.
PROVERBS 19:20 NIV

PERSONAL APPLICATION:

When you're faced with a big decision, it's tempting to talk to friends who are likely to cheer you on and tell you to go for it. But make sure you get advice from a variety of people who can provide insight and help you think through your decision from different perspectives. Seek out seasoned, mature believers who have a strong walk with God and consistently display wisdom and discernment in their own lives.

Waiting on God is one of the most essential aspects of decision-making. Ultimately, once we've sought wise counsel from others, we need clarity from God. When you're making an important decision, don't rush. Take time to slow down and seek the Lord for direction. As you read your Bible each day, ask God to speak to you through His Word and direct your steps.

PRAYER FOR TODAY:

Heavenly Father, thank You for guiding me on Your paths. I confess that I sometimes rush my decisions and don't give people the chance to speak into my life. I want to open myself up to the advice of others. Lead me to godly counselors who can give me biblical insight and perspective. As I wait on You and pray over the decisions I need to make, please give me great clarity and peace: [your prayer]. In Jesus' name, amen.

And your ears shall hear a word behind you, saying, "This is the way, walk in it," when you turn to the right or when you turn to the left.

ISAIAH 30:21 ESV

Day 32

HEARTS LIKE FLOWERS

———◦•◦———

He gathers the lambs in his arms
and carries them close to his heart.

ISAIAH 40:11 NIV

> *Hearts, like flowers, cannot be rudely handled, but must open naturally.*
>
> [CHAPTER 32]

When Marmee becomes anxious about Beth's low "spirits," she notices that Beth "sits alone a good deal, and doesn't talk to her father as much as she used." She cries over the babies, sings only sad songs, and has a "look in her face" that Marmee can't understand. Marmee asks Jo to try to find out what's wrong: "I leave Beth to your hands, then, for she will open her tender little heart to her Jo sooner than to anyone else."

As Jo determines to settle "Bethy's troubles," she sees that Marmee is right—something *is* wrong with Beth. And though she comes to the wrong conclusions at first, the way Jo comes alongside Beth provides a loving picture of the care that delicate situations and tender hearts require. In a particularly touching moment, Jo hears a "stifled sob" one night that makes her "fly to Beth's bedside, with the anxious inquiry, 'What is it, dear?' " She asks if she should call Mother, but Beth says no and asks Jo to lie beside her.

As Jo gently soothes "Beth's hot forehead and wet eyelids," her heart is "very full" and she longs to speak. But Jo has learned "that hearts, like flowers, cannot be rudely handled, but must open naturally." She can tell Beth is in pain, and she thinks she knows why, but she simply asks if it would comfort her to share her troubles. Jo assures Beth that she and Marmee "are always glad to hear and help." Beth isn't yet ready to share her burden, but she is comforted by Jo's presence and falls asleep.

When we're in deep pain or conflict, sometimes we need a gentle comforter more than anything else. We might not need advice or solutions. We may not be ready to open up. But it's a beautiful gift when a kind friend comes along and is happy just to "be" with you. There's nothing like having someone sit quietly with you when your heart is aching. To have someone hold your hand. To be loved and hugged, calmed and soothed.

Jesus invites you to bring all your troubles to Him because He is "gentle and humble in heart" (Matthew 11:29 NIV). The Bible tells us that when Jesus saw crowds of people, "he had compassion on them because they were confused and helpless, like sheep without a shepherd" (Matthew 9:36 NLT). When people came to Him for help, He didn't press them to confess their sins or share their problems. He asked questions, He leaned in and listened, and He spoke life into their situations. People opened their hearts to Him because they knew they could trust Him.

"Learn from Me, for I am gentle and lowly in heart."
MATTHEW 11:29 NKJV

PERSONAL APPLICATION:

Can you imagine the gentle hand of Jesus touching your drooped shoulders or weary head? What a wonderful comfort to know that Jesus is with us and loves us. When you need someone to lean on, He is always there. He knows your deepest aches and heaviest burdens. He can comfort and soothe your heart better than anyone else. As you pray today, ask Jesus to move the mountains you can't climb and split the seas you can't cross.

Hearts, like flowers, cannot be rushed to open. It takes time to gain someone's trust. If you know someone who is hurting, pray about the best way to be a kind and steady friend. It's a gift to know when to speak, when to listen, and when to just be.

PRAYER FOR TODAY:

Lord Jesus, I lift up to You today my own heartache and pain. I bring to You my burdens that seem too heavy, the wounds that hurt and won't heal. Be my gentle comforter. Help me to know You are near. And please show me how to share Your comfort with others. Teach me to be a good friend to people who are hurting. I want to set aside this time now to pray for other people and lift up their burdens to You. I pray especially for my friends who are struggling with heartache or weariness right now: [specific names]. In Jesus' name, amen.

The Sovereign Lord has given me his words of wisdom, so that I know how to comfort the weary.

ISAIAH 50:4 NLT

Day 33

NEW HORIZONS

"If you are faithful in little things, you will be faithful in large ones."

LUKE 16:10 NLT

> "A fine view and a church tower opposite atone for the many stairs, and I took a fancy to my den on the spot."
>
> [CHAPTER 33]

Away from home and working as a governess, Jo feels "at home at once, even in that big house full of strangers." Jo's room is a "funny little sky parlor," but she takes a "fancy" to her "den on the spot." There's a stove and a "nice table in a sunny window" where she can sit and write. Her "fine view" and "a church tower opposite" make it the perfect "nest." When she feels "a little bit homesick," she goes downstairs for dinner where "it's such fun to watch people."

For companionship Jo forms bonds with Mrs. Kirke, Professor Bhaer and his pupils, her own students, and the "rich, cultivated, and kind" Miss Norton. During Jo's work hours, she teaches and sews in a "pleasant room" off of Mrs. Kirke's private parlor and listens in on the professor and his pupils. She joins in with the delightful fun of learning and play instigated by Bhaer on school days and the "riotous times" to be had on Saturdays.

This little glimpse of Jo's future happiness and life's work won't come to fruition for a while—when she'll have a home of her own, a husband and children, a school full of boys to teach, and a full-fledged nest to feather. But for now she gets a taste of what is to come as she carves out a niche for herself where she's happy, comfortable, and needed. She finds she's well suited to teaching, studying, reading, writing, caring for lively children, and even mending and sewing.

God often uses the simple details of today to prepare us for tomorrow. Each season is part of a bigger picture as we learn and grow. Sometimes we find ourselves doing things that seem insignificant, but God can even bring side roads and detours into focus later on. As you dig in and do the tasks God has given you to do—with purpose and zeal—invite Him to mold you, shape you, and cause your work to flourish and expand. He can take the tiniest corner and carve out a place for you to start doing the work He has called you to do.

In the New Testament the apostle Paul was always learning, growing, and expanding his ministry. No matter where he was—whether he was there for a year, a few weeks, or just a few days—he never stopped doing God's work. He experienced shipwreck, hunger, cold, nakedness, beatings, and imprisonment (2 Corinthians 11:23–27). But everywhere he went, Paul settled in and got to work. Even in prison under constant surveillance by Roman guards, he lived out God's call on his life to teach and preach. As he worked willingly, God blessed his efforts abundantly.

Work willingly at whatever you do, as though you were working for the Lord rather than for people.
Colossians 3:23 nlt

PERSONAL APPLICATION:

No matter where you live, whether it's in a large house, a small apartment, a borrowed loft, or a shared room, work to make your little corner of the world friendly, inviting, and cheerful. Be faithful in the small things. Do everything with purpose and honor, as though you're working for God (Colossians 3:23).

Have you caught a glimpse of something God might be calling you to do? Don't be afraid to start small. Work hard and learn all you can right where you are today. Take an interest in the people around you, try new things, and get involved with helping at your church and in your community. God *will* use your today to impact your tomorrow.

———◦◦◦———

PRAYER FOR TODAY:

Thank You, Lord, for reminding me to be faithful and diligent with what You've put in front of me to do. I want to be hardworking, content, and cheerful in my daily work. Show me where I can do the most amount of good. May my work flourish and bear fruit. Help me notice needs and join with other believers to do Your work. Teach, mold, and shape me. Please speak to me about the future, and prepare my heart for all You have for me: [your prayer]. In Jesus' name, amen.

"For I know the plans I have for you," declares the Lord, "plans to prosper you and not to harm you, plans to give you hope and a future."
JEREMIAH 29:11 NIV

Day 34

GUARD
THE GATES

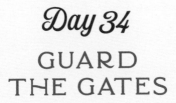

*"I looked for someone among them
who would build up the wall and stand
before me in the gap on behalf of the land."*
EZEKIEL 22:30 NIV

> *Somehow, as he talked, the world got right again to Jo. The old beliefs, that had lasted so long, seemed better than the new. God was not a blind force, and immortality was not a pretty fable, but a blessed fact. She felt as if she had solid ground under her feet again.*
>
> [CHAPTER 34]

Jo finds a true friend in Professor Bhaer—a friend who steadies her faith in two crucial moments. First, when a philosophy debate turns her mind "adrift into time and space, like a young balloon out on a holiday," though it costs him "an effort to speak," he defends God and biblical truth. The world is set "right" for Jo, and she finds "solid ground" once more.

Later, when he discovers Jo is writing sensational stories, Bhaer "does not say to himself: 'It is none of my business. I've no right to say anything.'" Instead, he feels "moved to help her" and speaks to her "quite naturally, but very gravely." Jo realizes that she has "gone blindly on, hurting [her]self and other people, for the sake of money" and decides to use her writing talents for a higher purpose from then on.

In both cases, Jo's own inner voice of conscience is muffled by worldly voices and influences. She knows the right way to go, but she gets swept up in new, heady experiences and ideas. At each juncture, Professor Bhaer sets up guideposts for her feet and sheds much-needed light on her path. She recognizes that the "old beliefs, that had lasted so long" are better than all the new philosophies she has heard, and she grows stronger in her personal faith.

We all need people who will speak up and speak into our lives when our feet stray from God's paths. It's important to have gatekeepers and standard-bearers who will stand up for righteousness and truth. When we become captivated by new ideas, we often don't notice the slow drift away from the solid foundation of our faith. We need people to speak truth and lead us back to God's paths.

Throughout Paul's epistles, he corrects, rebukes, warns, and exhorts. Why? Because we need constant reminders of God's truth in a world full of slippery slopes and cleverly disguised lies. There is a wide path that leads to destruction and a narrow path that leads to life (Matthew 7:13–14). There are wolves in sheep's clothing (Matthew 7:15) and "teachers who will tell [us] whatever [our] itching ears want to hear" (2 Timothy 4:3 NLT). We need to know the truth and always be on our guard.

That we may no longer be children,
tossed to and fro by the waves and
carried about by every wind of doctrine.

EPHESIANS 4:14 ESV

PERSONAL APPLICATION:

Do you find yourself getting carried away by new ideas and spiritual trends? One way you can keep your feet solidly planted in the truth is through regular Bible study and fellowship with mature believers. Studying God's Word and learning to apply it alongside knowledgeable teachers will keep you from getting tossed back and forth by every new wind of doctrine (Ephesians 4:14).

God is also calling you to be a gatekeeper and a prayer warrior in this generation. People are easily led astray by false doctrines, teachers, and philosophies that merely tickle the ears but aren't grounded in scripture (2 Timothy 4:3). We need to know what the Bible says, speak the truth in love, and help other believers stay the course.

———◦◆◦———

PRAYER FOR TODAY:

Lord God, I want to be alert and guard my faith carefully.
I desire to live by Your standards. Help me notice when
I'm getting caught up in new ideas or distracted by faulty
doctrine. Please grant me special discernment, and make
me into a wise and loving gatekeeper for others. Show me
if I've wavered or stepped off Your paths of righteousness.
I especially pray for this person who is struggling with
questions of faith: [specific name(s)]. In Jesus' name, amen.

"Stand at the crossroads and look; ask for the
ancient paths, ask where the good way is, and
walk in it, and you will find rest for your souls."

JEREMIAH 6:16 NIV

Day 35
CRUSHED

———◦◆◦———

*The LORD is near to the brokenhearted
and saves the crushed in spirit.*
PSALM 34:18 ESV

> "I don't know why I can't love you as you want me to. I've tried, but I can't change the feeling, and it would be a lie to say I do when I don't."
>
> [CHAPTER 35]

When Laurie graduates, he finally tells Jo he loves her. She tries to stop him, not wanting to have the conversation, not wanting to break his heart. But Laurie won't let her run away or evade the subject, saying, "It's no use, Jo, we've got to have it out, and the sooner the better for both of us." When Jo tells him that she doesn't love him in the same way, she feels as though she has "stabbed her dearest friend."

Jo hates to hurt "her boy," but she knows she must be honest. Delaying the truth would be "both useless and cruel." From the moment she says no to his proposal, Jo is faced with the terrible pain of wounding her best friend. When he leaves for Europe "without a look behind him," she knows that "the boy Laurie" will never "come again." The whole situation is so difficult that she barely has "the strength of mind to hold fast" to her resolution.

For Laurie, everything about this moment is excruciating. He has loved and looked up to Jo since they first met. He has "worked hard to please" her in school, he has given up billiards and "everything" Jo doesn't like, and he has "waited and never complained." All of his high hopes are dashed, and nothing he can say will change how she feels. In the pain of the moment, he declares he'll never get over her. He can't see how things could ever possibly turn out for good.

We all have personal experience with the pain of heartbreak, rejection, and disappointment. We've all had things we've hoped for, worked toward, and tried hard to get. We've had doors slammed in our faces and dreams that never came true. We've tried to change things that are impossible to change. We've loved people who didn't love us back. Above all, we've all had times when we've struggled to understand and accept God's timing, course corrections, and will for our lives.

When Paul and his team were in Phrygia and Galatia, they were "forbidden by the Holy Spirit to preach the word in Asia" (Acts 16:6 NKJV). They tried again in Mysia, but "the Spirit did not permit them" to go on (v. 7 NKJV). At Troas, the Lord gave Paul a vision in the night and sent him to Macedonia instead. Later God *did* send Paul to preach in Ephesus for two years, "so that all who dwelt in Asia heard the word of the Lord Jesus" (Acts 19:10 NKJV), but God knew the best timing and the best path for Paul to take.

And we know that God causes everything to work
together for the good of those who love God and
are called according to his purpose for them.
ROMANS 8:28 NLT

PERSONAL APPLICATION:

Have you had your hopes dashed or your heart crushed? Take it all to Jesus and ask Him to comfort you and guide you. "The LORD is near to the brokenhearted and saves the crushed in spirit" (Psalm 34:18 ESV). God knows the beginning from the end of your life. Allow Him to direct your paths and reveal His best for you. Seek Him daily, and ask Him to open your eyes to what better things He may have in store for you.

Laurie thought Jo would be his perfect companion, but he ultimately finds someone who complements his life and family far better. The same is true for Jo, who finds the perfect match for her personality and ambitions. When the things you want most don't come to fruition, be patient with what God is doing. His plans are far bigger and better than you can imagine.

───◦◆◦───

PRAYER FOR TODAY:

Lord Jesus, thank You for reminding me that unanswered prayers are sometimes for my good. I lift to You my dearest dreams and ask You to guide my steps. If You say no, I will trust You. If You ask me to wait, I will. If You want to redirect my paths, please make it clear. I invite You to shift my focus and bring me to something even more profitable wherever needed. As I wait, please heal the crushed feelings I've experienced in this situation: [your prayer]. In Jesus' name, amen.

Now all glory to God, who is able, through his mighty power at work within us, to accomplish infinitely more than we might ask or think.
EPHESIANS 3:20 NLT

Day 36
BY THE SEA

Share each other's burdens.
GALATIANS 6:2 NLT

> "Oh, Beth, and you didn't tell me, didn't let me comfort and help you? How could you shut me out, bear it all alone?"
>
> [CHAPTER 36]

When she comes home in the spring Jo is struck by the "change in Beth". Beth's face has a "strange, transparent look about it, as if the mortal was being slowly refined away." No one else in the family says anything about Beth's declining health, for it has "come too gradually to startle those who [see] her daily." But as Jo observes Beth carefully, the truth is "very plain" to Jo, and a "heavy weight" falls on her heart.

When the two sisters go to the seaside, it's clear that Beth is fading quickly. The fresh sea air and sunshine do little to strengthen her. Her hands seem "too feeble to hold even the rosy little shells" they collect. Jo knows Beth is "slowly drifting away from her." As they sit together on the sand, she holds Beth close. Beth finally tells Jo she knows she's dying, saying, "Jo, dear, I'm glad you know it. I've tried to tell you, but I couldn't."

In the tender scenes that follow, Beth explains that she has known for "a good while" and is at peace. Fierce Jo says she'll work and fight and pray to make Beth well again, but Beth would rather face reality together as best they can. Her quiet, childlike faith gives her the "courage and patience" she needs to "try to be willing." She comforts Jo, saying, "We'll have happy times, for I don't suffer much, and I think the tide will go out easily, if you help me."

This chapter reminds us that we aren't meant to carry our burdens alone. First, we need to let God in and allow Him to strengthen and comfort us. He is big enough and strong enough for *all* our troubles. Truly, there is no burden that is too heavy for God. Second, it's important to share our burdens with other people. When we sit together, hold hands, and talk and cry over our cares and concerns, we grow closer together and share sweet communion. As we invite others into our struggles, it creates deeper bonds and provides immense relief. There's something so helpful and healing about getting hard things out in the open.

First Peter 5:7 (NIV) tell us this: "Cast *all* your anxiety on him because he cares for you" (emphasis mine). Throughout the Bible, we find people who ran to God with their problems. In fact, Moses cried out to the Lord all the time! Every time he had a problem, he called out for help (Exodus 15 and 17). Moses knew that God alone possessed the wisdom and power needed to solve the giant issues that came with trying to lead an entire nation—and he understood he could never do it alone. Moses knew he needed God and wasn't afraid to ask for help.

> *Give your burdens to the Lord,*
> *and he will take care of you.*
> PSALM 55:22 NLT

PERSONAL APPLICATION:

You aren't meant to walk alone, toting your burdens around by yourself. God has given you friends, relatives, and the body of Christ to come alongside you in your difficulties. Galatians 6:2 teaches us to carry each other's burdens as members of God's family. As you share your troubles, others will feel more comfortable sharing theirs too. You can pray together and support one another through tough times and rough patches.

If someone you know is carrying a heavy burden, consider planning some time away together. Pack a picnic lunch and go to the park, watch a favorite movie together, or even plan a day trip or a mini staycation. There's nothing like getting away from our everyday routine to help us gain perspective and lighten our spirits.

———◦◆◦———

PRAYER FOR TODAY:

Dear Jesus, thank You for inviting me to give you all of my anxieties, worries, and burdens. Please show me the weights I'm carrying that I need to bring to You or share with a loved one. Open my eyes to the people around me who need a kind, supporting, and prayerful friend. Help me to be a safe and trustworthy confidant. Lord, I give You my burdens today and leave them in Your capable hands: [your prayer]. In Jesus' name, amen.

Cast all your anxiety on him
because he cares for you.
1 Peter 5:7 niv

Day 37

NEW EYES
TO SEE

———◦◆◦———

"Behold, I am making all things new."
REVELATION 21:5 ESV

> [Laurie] very naturally fell to studying [Amy] from this new point of view, and before the evening was half over, had decided that "little Amy" was going "to make a very charming woman."
>
> [CHAPTER 37]

When Laurie and Amy see one another in Europe, Amy finds something "missing" in "Laurie's manner," but she can't tell what. Though he is "handsomer than ever and greatly improved," he looks "tired and spiritless." Amy thinks he seems "older and graver than a year or two of prosperous life should have made him." She doesn't like his "indifferent" tone and thinks to herself, "If that's the way he's going to grow up, I wish he'd stay a boy."

As for Laurie, he notices that Amy is now mature, grown-up, and self-assured. He finds "nothing to perplex or disappoint" and "much to admire and approve." Amy is "sprightly and graceful" with the addition of "that indescribable something in dress and bearing which we call elegance." She has now "gained a certain aplomb in both carriage and conversation" and her "native frankness" has been "unspoiled by foreign polish." However, he still thinks of her like a little sister.

That evening something changes for them both. Amy dresses up with Laurie in mind and finds herself trying to catch his attention. Laurie admires Amy's dancing, speech, and pretty ensemble. When she finishes dancing a set, he has a "waked-up look" as he stands to give her his seat. He fills Amy's dance card with his name and "devote[s] himself to her for the rest of the evening in the most delightful manner."

Seeing people in a new light isn't always easy. Often we relate to people based on past experiences and first impressions. We assume they'll never change and things will always stay the same. But people do have the capacity to change and grow, especially under the influence of the Holy Spirit. Our God is in the business of making all things new and He is continually at work in your life and in the lives of your friends and loved ones. He can bring about profound changes in even the most difficult situations and relationships.

When Saul (later Paul) was radically saved and lost his sight on the road to Damascus, the Lord told a disciple named Ananias to go visit him (Acts 9). Ananias was understandably concerned because Saul had a reputation for persecuting Christians. But the Lord told Ananias that Saul was His chosen vessel, so he went and laid hands on Saul. Saul received the Holy Spirit, regained his sight, and was baptized. Both men probably stood there looking at each other with brand-new eyes! Formerly strangers and adversaries, they were suddenly brothers in Christ.

"My thoughts are nothing like your thoughts,"
says the LORD. "And my ways are far beyond
anything you could imagine."
ISAIAH 55:8 NLT

PERSONAL APPLICATION:

Whom or what do you need to see with new eyes? As you pray today, position yourself to look at things from God's point of view. Ask for the mind of Christ so you can see your circumstances and the people in your life from a different angle. God's thoughts are nothing like our thoughts; His ways are beyond anything we can imagine (Isaiah 55:8). Ask Him to do what only He can do—ask Him to make your blind eyes see.

Sometimes the very thing we want or need is right in front of us. Other times we waste time knocking on one door that's locked, all the while missing the opportunity to walk through another one that is wide open. If you want to get on board with what God is doing, start praying for a breakthrough and for new eyes to see. Get input from other Christians and pay close attention. Open yourself up to fresh perspectives and allow God to do a new work!

PRAYER FOR TODAY:

Lord, thank You for making all things new. I know You are in the business of rebuilding, reshaping, and renewing the whole world. I confess that I often see people and situations at face value, not as You see them. Please renew my way of thinking and seeing. Open my eyes and take off any blinders. Change my heart and give me the mind of Christ for the following people and situations: [your prayer]. In Jesus' name, amen.

---

*"Be strong and courageous. Do not be afraid; do not be discouraged, for the L*ORD* your God will be with you wherever you go."*

JOSHUA 1:9 NIV

Day 38

WORN DOWN AND WEARY

He refreshes my soul.
PSALM 23:3 NIV

> [Meg] was nervous and worn
> out with watching and worry.
>
> [CHAPTER 38]

In this chapter exhausted new mother Meg inadvertently makes "the mistake that most young wives make." She has "forgotten" her husband in her "love" for her children. She has become "absorbed" by the twins "to the utter exclusion of everything and everybody else." She broods over them "with tireless devotion and anxiety, leaving John to the tender mercies of the help." She becomes increasingly "worn and nervous" as the twins take "every minute of her time."

As for John, he is "very uncomfortable, for the children [have] bereft him of his wife, home [is] merely a nursery and the perpetual 'hushing' [makes] him feel like a brutal intruder whenever he enter[s] the sacred precincts of Babyland." Meg shoos him away, taking on the full burden of parenting and leaving John without a role to play. Feeling lonely and unwanted at home, John starts having supper at a friend's house.

When Meg finally opens up to her mother, Marmee says Meg has made a "very natural and forgivable mistake," but it's one that "had better be remedied" sooner than later. She proposes wise and practical solutions, telling Meg to let John take his part in the parenting, allow Hannah to help with the twins, and stop confining herself to the nursery. She says she should go out more, get some exercise, and take an interest in John and the world outside her door. Her final word of advice is this: "Keep cheerful as well as busy, for you are the sunshine-maker of the family, and if you get dismal there is no fair weather."

We each have the opportunity to be sunshine-makers in our homes and communities, but we can't do that if we're running on empty. If you're constantly overwhelmed and rushed, it's impossible to stay cheerful, notice needs, and nurture loving relationships. We all need balance in our lives—both spiritually and physically. We need to take walks, engage with the outside world, make time for friends, and allow others to share the work. And most importantly, we need time to sit at Jesus' feet each day.

In the biblical account of Mary and Martha in Luke 10 (ESV), Jesus showed Martha that she was "anxious and troubled about many things," but that only "one thing" was "necessary": time spent with Him (vv. 41–42). He didn't say that to shame Martha. He also didn't say she shouldn't work hard or share her wonderful gift of hospitality. He merely helped shift Martha's focus from everyone else's physical needs to her own spiritual needs—He didn't want her confined to the kitchen and her work. He knew that her soul needed to be fed.

> *"Martha, Martha, you are anxious and troubled about many things, but one thing is necessary."*
> LUKE 10:41–42 ESV

PERSONAL APPLICATION:

Is one area of your life threatening to take over everything else? Take this time to quiet your heart and sit at Jesus' feet. Look at your to-do list and ask God to show you what to delegate, save for later, or cross off altogether. Get outside and take a walk or check in on a neighbor. Breathe deeply and invite Jesus to refresh your spirit.

Sometimes we get so wrapped up in all of the things we have to do each day—even serving God—that we lose sight of the people around us. If you know someone who works long hours, has a new baby, or is caring for someone with special needs, take a break from your own projects and think of one practical thing you can do this week to help them out. And if you're feeling overwhelmed, don't try to do it all alone. Let other people help.

———◦◆◦———

PRAYER FOR TODAY:

Lord Jesus, please help me to see the things that are taking too much of my time and attention. Open my eyes to the relationships that need tending and cross unnecessary things off my list. Fill me anew with Your Holy Spirit, and show me where to adjust my focus. Give me creative ideas for how to help someone who is worn down and weary. Please order my steps and help me find balance in this area of my life: [your prayer]. In Jesus' name, amen.

*Those who hope in the LORD
will renew their strength.*

ISAIAH 40:31 NIV

Day 39
GET MOVING

"Take heart. Get up;
he is calling you."
MARK 10:49 ESV

In this chapter it's Amy who gives a lesson and a lecture to someone who is hurting but in great need of a wake-up call: her dear friend Theodore Laurence. After Jo's rejection, Laurie has been wandering around Europe doing nothing much. He has kept his hurt hidden and hasn't told anyone of his great disappointment. Running from the pain, he has done nothing to further his career, his art, or his character. Worse yet, he has become bitter and indifferent.

Amy becomes fed up with seeing Laurie waste precious time and resources. Finally, "longing to see him shake off the apathy that so altered him," she sharpens "both tongue and pencil" and tells him the hard truth: "With every chance for being good, useful, and happy, you are faulty, lazy, and miserable." She says he has "grown abominably lazy," likes gossip, and wastes his time on "frivolous things." She doesn't like this new Laurie who is "contented to be petted and admired by silly people, instead of being loved and respected by wise ones."

Amy, who has learned to make so much out of so little, can't understand how Laurie, "with money, talent, position, health, and beauty"—and with so many "splendid things to use and enjoy"—can find nothing to do "but dawdle." When she finally gets to the root of the problem, her tone changes. She shows great compassion for his broken heart, but her advice is still in the same vein: "Love Jo all your days, if you choose, but don't let it spoil you." She says, "It's wicked to throw away so many good gifts because you can't have the one you want."

A great disappointment or sorrow can often cause us to fall into a kind of stupor. We have a tendency to run away, lose interest in things, or become bitter. But while we do need time to process heartache, it's unhealthy to get stuck there and dwell on our problems. God always has more in store for us; there is always another door to open. With or without the desires of our heart being met, there comes a time when we need to get up and get moving again.

After King Saul disobeyed the Lord, the Bible tells us that the prophet Samuel never went to see Saul again. He mourned for Saul and was greatly grieved (1 Samuel 15:35). But God didn't leave Samuel to wallow forever. In fact, He asked Samuel: "How long will you mourn for Saul, seeing I have rejected him from reigning over Israel?" (1 Samuel 16:1 NKJV). You see, God had more work for Samuel to do. All was not lost. Samuel's days as a prophet were not over. And when God told Samuel to get up and go anoint a new king, Samuel went!

> *"Fill your horn with oil, and go."*
> 1 SAMUEL 16:1 NKJV

PERSONAL APPLICATION:

God is the lifter of your head (Psalm 3:3). He wants to give you a renewed sense of hope—in Him and in His promises. Ecclesiastes 3:4 (ESV) says there is "a time to weep, and a time to laugh; a time to mourn, and a time to dance." If you've been experiencing a season of sadness, ask Jesus to bring you into a new season of joy.

Perhaps God is telling you it's time to get moving again. If you're feeling stuck, seek out friends who love you but won't let you wallow. Try something new. Take a class or sign up for a 5K walk for charity. Tune up your bike, dust off a musical instrument, or help in your church office. While you're at it, invite a friend to join you!

PRAYER FOR TODAY:

Lord Jesus, thank You for showing me where I'm languishing and stuck. Please wake me up and shake me up and get me moving again. I need Your help to shift my focus away from my problems and onto other things. Renew my hope and replenish my joy. I believe You have much more in store for me, and I want to get on board with what You want to do next. Show me how to move forward in this area of my life: [your prayer]. In Jesus' name, amen.

I am sure of this, that he who began a good work in you will bring it to completion at the day of Jesus Christ.

PHILIPPIANS 1:6 ESV

Day 40

A LIFE
THAT SHINES

———⊙•⊙———

*I have fought the good fight, I have
finished the race, I have kept the faith.*
2 TIMOTHY 4:7 ESV

> *With eyes made clear by many tears,*
> *and a heart softened by the tenderest*
> *sorrow, [Jo] recognized the beauty of*
> *her sister's life—uneventful, unambitious,*
> *yet full of the genuine virtues which*
> *"smell sweet, and blossom in the dust."*
>
> [CHAPTER 40]

The first of Beth's final days are "very happy ones." The "pleas-antest room in the house" is filled with "everything that she most loved, flowers, pictures, her piano, the little worktable, and the beloved pussies." There, Marmee, Meg, and Jo sew, Father reads, and the babies play. She's surrounded by Father's books, Mother's chair, Jo's desk, Amy's sketches, fruit from John, gifts and letters from "across the sea," and Hannah's "dainty dishes."

Beth makes little gifts for the children walking by her window because "even while preparing to leave life, she trie[s] to make it happier for those who should remain behind." As she worsens, there are "such heavy days, such long, long nights, such aching hearts and imploring prayers." When the worst is over and she is at peace again, Beth's body is wrecked but her soul is strong. Her family knows she's ready—that "the first pilgrim called" is "likewise the fittest."

In these last days, as she stays by Beth's side day and night, Jo is forever changed. She watches Beth read her "well-worn little book" and hears her singing and quietly crying as she tries to "wean herself from the dear old life, and fit herself for the life to come, by sacred words of comfort, quiet prayers, and the music she loved so well." Observing Beth's "simple, unselfish way" does more for Jo than "the wisest sermons, the saintliest hymns, the most fervent prayers that any voice could utter."

Sometimes the greatest sermon we can preach is by the way we live, the way we love, the way we serve, and even by the way we suffer. In the hardest moments, through the struggle and the fight, when our faith is put to the test, that's when God's faithfulness is tested and proved. No one can meet every challenge with perfect patience and forbearance, but when we cling to Jesus, our souls grow strong and we find that He is enough.

The soldiers who guarded Paul in Rome couldn't help but observe him closely. He used his time to preach, pray, sing, and write letters. Everyone there knew he was in chains for his faith (Philippians 1:13). And yet Paul wrote this to the church at Philippi: "Rejoice in the Lord always; again I will say, rejoice." (Philippians 4:4 ESV). What a powerful testimony! Paul's guards witnessed his strong faith and continual joy—*despite* his circumstances. Even in the darkest times, Paul made it his aim to shine for Jesus.

> *"This is to my Father's glory, that you bear much fruit, showing yourselves to be my disciples."*
> JOHN 15:8 NIV

PERSONAL APPLICATION:

When we least expect it, our faith can make the most impact. It might be in a doctor's office or a hospital, while you're cooking or cleaning your kitchen for the tenth time in the same day, or when you show up for a friend in crisis. Your quiet, determined faith speaks volumes on the most ordinary of days and during life's hardest moments.

Perhaps you feel like you don't have a lot of influence or talent. Maybe you have physical limitations or poor health. God is not looking for the strongest or the brightest people to be His witnesses. You can help make life happier for others in many creative ways. Ask God to show you how to "let your light so shine before men, that they may see your good works and glorify your Father in heaven" (Matthew 5:16 NKJV).

PRAYER FOR TODAY:

Dearest Jesus, thank You for reminding me that You are working through me in ways I can't see or imagine. Make me Your vessel, that I might testify of Your love and shine for You all the days of my life. Open my eyes to see the divine appointments You have for me and help me make it a habit to pray and rejoice on the good days and the bad. Please show me how I can brighten someone else's life this week: [your prayer]. In Jesus' name, amen.

---

*[The Lord's] pleasure is not in the strength
of the horse, nor his delight in the legs of the
warrior; the LORD delights in those who fear him,
who put their hope in his unfailing love.*

PSALM 147:10–11 NIV

Day 41

ROWING
TOGETHER

*Two are better than one, because they
have a good reward for their toil.*
ECCLESIASTES 4:9 ESV

During Beth's illness, Laurie and Amy are both still abroad, each in different cities. Laurie, who thought the "task of forgetting his love for Jo would absorb all his powers for years," is surprised to find that it grows easier every day. He tries to make his heart ache, but it won't. Instead of "trying to forget," he finds himself "trying to remember." After he writes to Jo one last time, Laurie finds the closure he needs. He gathers up her letters and takes off her ring, locks both items in his desk, and goes out to hear High Mass.

Laurie begins writing to Amy, who is terribly homesick, and their correspondence flourishes "famously," with letters flying "to and fro with unfailing regularity all through the early spring." Amy declines Fred Vaughn's marriage proposal and begins to show signs of love for Laurie. She makes "charming little presents" for him and sends him letters full of news and gossip. As for *his* letters, Amy carries them in her pocket—crying over the short ones and kissing the long ones.

When the sad news of Beth's passing comes, Amy is distraught and far from home, wishing Laurie would come. As soon as he hears the news, he travels quickly to her side. With his dark head "bent down protectingly" over her light one, they find mutual comfort and love. Over the following weeks, they bear their "new sorrow" together, side by side. And one day, while rowing on the lake, Amy points out how well they row together—that they're stronger together than apart. Laurie says he wishes they "might always pull in the same boat" and tenderly asks Amy to marry him.

May this poignant picture of comfort and companionship be a reminder to you of Jesus' steadfast love for you. Jesus is *in* the boat with you. No matter where you go or what storms you face, you are never alone. When you can't row any further, when you're taking on water, when you feel like you might sink, He sticks closer than a brother (Proverbs 18:24). You never have to "pull" alone; He is always by your side.

God also sends others to row alongside us. In Ecclesiastes 4:9–12 (ESV), we learn that God has created us for human partnership: "Two are better than one, because they have a good reward for their toil." If one of them falls, the other will "lift up his fellow." When it's cold, two people can huddle together for warmth. And in the event of an attack, two can "withstand" an enemy together. In companionship with others, we bear more fruit, lift each other up, enjoy warm fellowship, and have each other's back.

There is a friend who sticks closer than a brother.
PROVERBS 18:24 NIV

PERSONAL APPLICATION:

Who has God put in your boat to row with you in this season? Take note of the people you see regularly, and make it a priority to continually seek out the companionship of people who are steadfast and serious about their faith. Choose your close friends, business partners, and romantic relationships wisely, remembering that the people you spend time with will impact your character and your fruitfulness for Christ.

When we row together in unison with others, we go further and last longer. But sometimes we need to pull for someone else. Laurie went straight to Amy in her time of grief and stayed by her side. You can do the same for the people you know and love. When someone is hurting or in need, there's nothing like a personal visit or a phone call from a faithful friend.

PRAYER FOR TODAY:

Jesus, thank You for this reminder that You are always by my side. I am so glad You are in my boat. Thank You for the way You walk with me through the storms of life and send people to row alongside me. Help me build deeper bonds with other Christians and enjoy rich fellowship together. Show me how to be a friend who sticks closer than a brother/sister to these people: [specific names]. In Jesus' name, amen.

He heals the brokenhearted
and binds up their wounds.
PSALM 147:3 ESV

Day 42

THE BITTER
AND THE SWEET

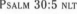

*Weeping may last through the night,
but joy comes with the morning.*
PSALM 30:5 NLT

> *Jo did not recognize her good angels at once because they wore familiar shapes and used the simple spells best fitted to poor humanity.*
>
> [CHAPTER 42]

After losing Beth, Jo feels she might "do something desperate" if somebody doesn't come and help her. Many loving "angels" and gentle "helps" surround her and carry her through her pain. Her mother comforts her heart, "not with words only, but the patient tenderness that soothes by a touch." They share "sacred moments," when "heart talked to heart in the silence of the night, turning affliction to a blessing." With Marmee's help, Jo's "aching heart" receives comfort and her life looks "more endurable, seen from the safe shelter of her mother's arms."

For her "troubled mind," Jo finds solace in long talks with her father, who welcomes her into his quiet study. She sits in Beth's little chair "close beside him" and tells him all her troubles. As he helps her, they both find "consolation in the act," enjoying "happy, thoughtful times" in what Jo calls the "church of one member." Jo comes away with "fresh courage, recovered cheerfulness, and a more submissive spirit."

And Jo is given other helps—"humble, wholesome duties and delights" in the form of "brooms and dishcloths," long talks with Meg, and playtime with the twins. But it's Marmee who sees Jo's restless, despondent spirit and suggests she start writing again: "Write something for us, and never mind the rest of the world." And so Jo begins to "scratch" away, finding renewed joy in writing her "simple stories," having now been "taught by love and sorrow." New life flows in as she finds her voice and begins to flourish as a writer.

Marmee tells Jo, "You have had the bitter, now comes the sweet." When we're in the midst of the bitter parts of life, it's hard to see God at work. We often feel aimless, lonely, and unsettled. However, some of the hardest times are followed by tender times of sweet renewal. Though it takes time, God does bring us back to life after a period of great loss. He brings consolation, comfort, and healing and leads us into new seasons of usefulness and creativity.

When work began on the new temple in Jerusalem after the Babylonian captivity, there was great joy mingled with great sorrow (Ezra 3). While many of the Jews cheered, the remnant who had seen the original temple in its former glory wept. However, in Zechariah 4:10 (NLT) we find this: "Do not despise these small beginnings, for the LORD rejoices to see the work begin, to see the plumb line in Zerubbabel's hand." Joy and sorrow sometimes go hand in hand. Even when it's bittersweet, we can rejoice in God's new beginnings.

I will be glad and rejoice in your love, for you saw
my affliction and knew the anguish of my soul.
PSALM 31:7 NIV

PERSONAL APPLICATION:

Are you in need of comfort? Have you experienced loss? God knows your affliction and anguish (Psalm 31:7 NIV). He will send comforters to help you, counselors to guide you, and "humble, wholesome duties and delights" to console you. Be assured that mourning lasts for a night, but joy *does come* in the morning (Psalm 30:5 NLT).

God also wants you to share His comfort with other people. 2 Corinthians 1:4 (ESV) says that God "comforts us in all our affliction, so that we may be able to comfort those who are in any affliction, with the comfort with which we ourselves are comforted by God." If you know someone who has suffered a loss, you can come alongside that person to pray, read scripture, and provide practical help.

PRAYER FOR TODAY:

Lord Jesus, thank You for sending Your Holy Spirit to guide and comfort me. Please surround me and supply me with plenty of good "helps" in this season. Lead me to the right people who can minister to my heart and my troubled mind. Help me to see Your good gifts all around me. Heal the bitter and usher in the sweet, I pray. I especially need Your healing touch in this area of my life: [your prayer]. In Jesus' name, amen.

*O LORD my God, I cried to you for help,
and you have healed me.*
PSALM 30:2 ESV

Day 43

A CORDIAL WELCOME

The Lord added to their number day by day those who were being saved.

ACTS 2:47 ESV

> *If the stranger had any doubts about his reception, they were set at rest in a minute by the cordial welcome he received.*
>
> [CHAPTER 43]

In this chapter Mr. Laurence and newlyweds Laurie and Amy arrive home after several years abroad. While Amy is down visiting Meg and the twins, Laurie and Jo have a good heart-to-heart, catching up on all the news and settling into a new rhythm together. They discover that even though they "can't be little playmates any longer," they will be "brother and sister" who "love and help one another" all their lives.

Once everyone is home together, there is great joy all around. It's a reunion full of warmth and stories: "Mercy on us, how they did talk! first one, then the other, then all burst out together—trying to tell the history of three years in half an hour." They make a "happy procession" as they file into the dining room for tea. Mr. Laurence accompanies Jo, saying, "You must be my girl now," with a glance at Beth's "empty corner by the fire."

After tea Jo feels "a sudden sense of loneliness," but a knock at the door brings a surprise visitor: Professor Bhaer. He receives a "cordial welcome," and everyone greets him kindly, first for "Jo's sake" and then "for his own." He fits in easily, and they all warm to him right away. After Hannah puts the twins to bed and

Mr. Laurence goes home to rest, the others sit "round the fire, talking away, utterly regardless of the lapse of time." Jo suggests they end the evening with a "sing, in the good old way, for we are all together again once more."

This reunion chapter provides a fitting picture of the family of God—where there's always room for more at the table. When we gather with like-hearted companions, our hearts swell with a sense of shared affections, common interests, and mutual love. Like the believers in the book of Acts, our circles of fellowship blossom and flourish in the common bond of our love for Jesus and a passion for serving God. And it's wonderful when new people join us and take their place at the table, filling in gaps and living out their unique roles in the body of Christ.

In 1 Corinthians 12:12–13 (NIV) Paul explains how the Church works in harmony: "Just as a body, though one, has many parts, but all its many parts form one body, so it is with Christ. For we were all baptized by one Spirit so as to form one body." Every believer fits together with other believers, each with a specific purpose. Together we are a healthy body; apart we cannot function correctly. God "put the body together" by design, so that "its parts should have equal concern for each other."

Now you are the body of Christ,
and each one of you is a part of it.
1 CORINTHIANS 12:27 NIV

PERSONAL APPLICATION:

There is always room for more people at God's fellowship table. Let's be the kind of Christians who extend a cordial welcome to strangers and invite visitors to join us in vibrant, authentic community. There are plenty of people who are looking for a place where they can fit and feel at home. Make it your goal to be the first to pull up an extra chair, widen the circle, and set another place at the table.

Are you longing for deeper fellowship with other Christians? Don't lose heart. There is a place at the table that can only be filled by you. If you're not sure where you fit, sign up to serve in a ministry at your church, join a small group, or attend a weekly prayer meeting. As you help, study, and pray with other believers, God will show you how and where to use your gifts.

PRAYER FOR TODAY:

Lord, thank You for showing me such a warm picture of togetherness with other believers. Please lead me to like-hearted companions and true fellowship with other Christians. Help me find where I fit, show me where to serve, and get me out of my comfort zone. Give me a heart for inviting people to the fellowship table. Show me how to make these people feel more welcome: [specific names]. In Jesus' name, amen.

"Go out into the country lanes and behind the hedges and urge anyone you find to come, so that the house will be full."
LUKE 14:23 NLT

Day 44

GENEROSITY
OF SPIRIT

—◦◦◦◦◦—

*Honor the L*ORD *with your wealth and with
the best part of everything you produce.*

PROVERBS 3:9 NLT

> *They hoped to brighten other homes,
> believing that their own feet would
> walk more uprightly along the flowery
> path before them, if they smoothed
> rough ways for other feet.*
>
> [CHAPTER 44]

As Laurie and Amy settle into married life together, Amy describes the "lovely weather" they've been enjoying as a couple, saying, "I don't know how long it will last, but I'm not afraid of storms, for I'm learning how to sail my ship." Indeed, they seem to be on the same page about most things, including how they want to live in regard to all they've been given.

On the topic of finances, they brainstorm ways to help Professor Bhaer, creatives and artists, and others who might need assistance. Amy says she has always wanted to have the "power of giving freely." Now, thanks to Laurie, her "dream has come true." She'd like to help "ambitious girls" who need "a little help at the right minute." Friends and relatives have been "very kind" to her, and she wants to "put out" her hand and do the same.

Laurie joins in, saying, "We'll do quantities of good, won't we?" While abroad, he saw many talented young men make "all sorts of sacrifices" and endure "real hardships" to "realize" their dreams. He'd like the "honor to be allowed to serve them." With a "glow of philanthropic zeal," he says, "It's not half so sensible to leave legacies when one dies as it is to use the money wisely while alive, and enjoy making one's fellow creatures happy with it."

Laurie and Amy make a wonderful discovery in this chapter: Life is much more pleasant when you share what you have with others than if you keep it all to yourself. And the beauty of giving is that you don't have to be wealthy to be generous. Generosity of spirit is about noticing needs and meeting them in your own way with what you have. As Jesus taught when He witnessed the widow giving her last two "mites" at the temple, it's not the amount that pleases God; it's the heart of the giver (Luke 21:1–4).

In Genesis 24 Abraham's servant went to Canaan to find a wife for Isaac. When he arrived, he stopped at a well and asked God to direct his steps: "May it be that when I say to a young woman, 'Please let down your jar that I may have a drink,' and she says, 'Drink, and I'll water your camels too'—let her be the one you have chosen" (v. 14 NIV). Just then Rebekah came to the well, offered him a drink, *and* watered all his camels! Abraham's servant wasn't impressed by Rebekah's wealth or beauty that day; he was struck by her generosity. She willingly served a stranger and gave him the best of what she had to give.

Each one must give as he has decided in
his heart, not reluctantly or under compulsion,
for God loves a cheerful giver.

2 Corinthians 9:7 ESV

PERSONAL APPLICATION:

Amy learned to give generously as a young girl when she had little to give, and it became a part of who she is. You too can create a habit of giving and make it part of your lifestyle. In a world that's all about "me" and what we can "get," generosity takes thought, intention, and practice. Sharing with others brings greater joy to the giver than to the receiver (Acts 20:35).

This week ask God to help you find ways to give of your own personal resources—of your time, your practical abilities, your treasure, and even your energy. God blesses us so that we can bless others. You can do things to lighten another person's load—even by carrying groceries up a flight of stairs, helping with administrative duties, providing a snack, or by doing a task without being asked.

———◦◦◦———

PRAYER FOR TODAY:

*Lord God, thank You for reminding me how much better
it is to give than receive. Help me form a habit of generosity,
and show me how I can give of my time, abilities, compassion,
finances, and practical knowledge to help others. Please make
me a vessel You can use to pour out into the lives of other
people. All that I have, I give to You. Open my eyes to the ways I
can be generous this week: [your prayer]. In Jesus' name, amen.*

*"Give, and it will be given to you. A good measure,
pressed down, shaken together and running over,
will be poured into your lap."*
LUKE 6:38 NIV

Day 45

TO ALL GENERATIONS

---

*One generation shall commend your works to
another, and shall declare your mighty acts.*

PSALM 145:4 ESV

> "These children are wiser than we are,
> and I have no doubt the boy understands
> every word I have said to him."
>
> [CHAPTER 45]

In this chapter about Daisy and Demi, we get an inspiring picture of what it looks like when loving people invest in a child's life. Introspective Daisy learns to "needle" and cook, setting up "housekeeping in the sideboard" and managing "a microscopic cooking stove with a skill that brings tears of pride to Hannah's eyes." Active and mechanical Demi learns "his letters with his grandfather" who invents a "new mode of teaching the alphabet by forming letters with his arms and legs."

The twins are surrounded by good and creative teachers: Their own parents watch over them, discipline them, and train them. Mr. and Mrs. March spend time with the children, teaching them all the lessons they taught their own girls. Aunt Dodo (Jo) is the "chief playmate and confidante of both children," a grown-up who still loves to play and turn "the little house topsy-turvy." And Mr. Bhaer soon becomes a favorite with both children as well.

But there are also many things the twins learn that aren't taught in lessons or words—things they see, perceive, and model by watching the adults in their family. They mimic their parents, grandparents, and aunts and uncle, trying to do things like the adults. They notice, they look, and they even find things out. With "infantile penetration," Demi realizes that Jo likes to "play 'with the bear-man' " (Mr. Bhaer) more than she likes to play with him and points out that "great boys like great girls, too," much to the surprise of everyone else.

No matter our age or situation in life, we're all teachers. The way we do things, the way we treat people, and the choices we make are all observed by the people around us. And we can either set a good example and lead people on right paths or we can go with the flow and lead people down side paths. This doesn't mean we have to be perfect; it just means that we try to live out our faith in practical ways, with kindness and care for others. It's as simple as being quick to ask forgiveness in a culture that has forgotten how to say "I'm sorry," by keeping our speech pure, by turning the other cheek, and by helping people without expecting anything in return.

We see the importance of teaching and training the next generation when we consider what happened to the Israelites after they entered the promised land: "After that generation died, another generation grew up who did not acknowledge the LORD or remember the mighty things he had done for Israel" (Judges 2:10 NLT). From there the Israelites spun out into idolatry and sinfulness for generations. They forgot all about what God had done for them—and they neglected to tell their children.

> *He commanded our ancestors to teach [God's laws]*
> *to their children, so the next generation might know*
> *them—even the children not yet born—and they*
> *in turn will teach their own children.*
> PSALM 78:5–6 NLT

PERSONAL APPLICATION:

The best way the next generation can know the Lord and remember all He has done is if this generation teaches them well. Whether you're married or single and whether you have siblings, grandchildren, nieces, nephews, or friends with children, you have the opportunity, pleasure, and responsibility to teach younger people to know and love God. There is no greater joy than helping other people learn to follow Jesus.

How do you teach others? You can tell stories from the Old and New Testament that illustrate the "mighty things" God has done for His people. You can share "God" stories from your life and the lives of other Christians, missionaries, and martyrs. You can even become a mentor, a sports coach, a youth leader, or a Sunday school teacher. No matter how you do it, be sure to pray for the younger people in your life, and help them to know and follow God.

PRAYER FOR TODAY:

Lord, thank You for the examples You've set before me in Your Word and in Your faithful followers. Train my eyes to look for godly role models for my own life and learn from them. Show me how to play a role in teaching the next generation to follow Jesus, and help me set a good example for the following people: [your prayer]. In Jesus' name, amen.

---

*Train up a child in the way he should go,
and when he is old he will not depart from it.*
PROVERBS 22:6 NKJV

Day 46

DEARER EVERY MINUTE

Nevertheless, I am continually with you;
you hold my right hand.
PSALM 73:23 ESV

> "Be worthy, love,
> and love will come."
>
> [CHAPTER 46]

On Jo's walks to Meg's house each evening, she always meets Mr. Bhaer "either going or returning," no matter which path she takes. After two weeks, everyone in the family knows "perfectly well" what's going on, but they all try to appear "stone-blind" to the changes in her face. While Bhaer talks "philosophy with the father" during his evening visits, he also gives "the daughter lessons in love."

As for Jo, she can't seem to "lose her heart in a decorous manner" and "sternly" tries to "quench" her feelings. She leads a "somewhat agitated life" as Mr. Bhaer becomes to her "dearer every minute." She sings while she works, puts her hair up "three times a day," and looks as though she's "blooming." And when they meet on a rainy walk one evening and shop together, Jo realizes she's falling "very fast."

When Mr. Bhaer says he loves her, Jo is overjoyed. She can't stop herself from asking "confidential questions" because he gives such "delightful answers." He admits that a line in her poem—"Be worthy, love, and love will come"—gave him reason to hope. She tells him he is "the one precious thing" she needs, and they become engaged right there in the dripping rain. When he says he can only offer her "a full heart" and "empty hands," Jo puts both of her hands into his, saying, "Not empty now," and kisses him.

You are "dearer every minute" to your loving heavenly Father, who has a heart full of love for you and hands always outstretched to you. Throughout the New Testament, Jesus touched people who needed healing and salvation. And the same is true for you. No matter how long you've walked with Jesus—or even if today is the first day you find yourself calling out to Him—He is there to hold your hands and walk with you through every minute of your life.

When Peter and John went to the temple to pray, they met a man who was "lame from birth" and asking for alms (Acts 3:2 ESV). Peter told him, "I have no silver and gold, but what I do have I give to you. In the name of Jesus Christ of Nazareth, rise up and walk!" (v. 6 ESV). Peter took the man's hand—and he stood up and began to walk and leap and praise God! Though you may not have any silver or gold, your hands are *never* empty with Jesus. You carry a gift that is beyond all earthly treasure—one that is meant to be shared with as many people as possible.

"For God so loved the world that he gave his
one and only Son, that whoever believes in
him shall not perish but have eternal life."
JOHN 3:16 NIV

PERSONAL APPLICATION:

Is Jesus becoming dearer to you all the time? How has your life changed for the better since you started walking hand-in-hand with Him? If you have become distant from Him in any way, take this time to return to your first love with all your heart. Ask Jesus to renew your passion for Him and revive you. He is right there beside you. Turn to Him and get swept up in His love all over again.

Perhaps you don't know Jesus very well yet—or at all. Today He is standing at the door of your heart, offering you His love, forgiveness, and salvation. All you have to do is take His hand. If you'd like to know more about how to have a personal relationship with Jesus, please go to "An Invitation" on page 221.

PRAYER FOR TODAY:

Dear Jesus, thank You for loving me and saving me. Thank You for holding my hand through all of life's beauty and struggle. I want to walk closer to You every day and get to know You even more. I love You, and I need You. Please move in my heart today to show me where I might be walking at a distance from Your love. I ask You now for personal revival in this part of my life and faith: [your prayer]. In Jesus' name, amen.

---

*And I am convinced that nothing
can ever separate us from God's love.*

ROMANS 8:38 NLT

Day 47

A BOUNTIFUL HARVEST

———◆———

*I have no greater joy than to hear that
my children are walking in the truth.*

3 JOHN 4 ESV

> *"We never can thank you enough for the patient sowing and reaping you have done,"* cried Jo, *with the loving impetuosity which she never would outgrow.*
>
> [CHAPTER 47]

On Apple Picking Day at Plumfield, we get to witness another "harvest"—of all the fruit that's come from years of faithful sowing—in the lives of the March family. The March girls are still on their pilgrimage and yet so much further along. Jo is in her element with Frederick and their boys. Meg thanks God for her little home and family, declaring herself "the happiest woman in the world." And Amy, now the mother of one "frail" daughter named Beth, continues to grow "sweeter, deeper, and more tender" in character.

When the apple picking is done, Jo and Meg set out "supper on the grass, for an out-of-door tea." There are cookies, apple turnovers, games of leapfrog, and tea party activities for the little girls. In honor of Marmee's sixtieth birthday, the children present "the queen of the day with various gifts, so numerous that they [are] transported to the festive scene in a wheelbarrow." As a grand finale, the boys sing a song from the treetops that Jo wrote and Laurie set to music.

Afterward Father enjoys the day, walking and talking in the sunshine with Professor Bhaer, and Marmee sits "enthroned among her daughters, with their children in her lap and at her feet." Her girls thank her for all the "patient sowing and reaping" she has done. Nearly speechless, with her arms open wide and her "face and voice full of motherly love, gratitude, and humility," she can only say, "Oh, my girls, however long you may live, I never can wish you a greater happiness than this!"

This touching ending reminds us that there's nothing in this life more precious or worthwhile than investing in the hearts and souls of people. The apostle John wrote, "I have no greater joy than to hear that my children are walking in the truth" (3 John 1:4 ESV). Truly, no joy compares to that of helping people grow in their faith and seeing them flourish and pass it on. Regardless of your station in life—whether you're young or old, single or married, with or without children—Jesus has called you to sow, plant, and water spiritual seeds.

During His earthly ministry, Jesus patiently sowed into hearts and lives and gave His life as a ransom for many (Matthew 20:28). Everywhere He went He invited people to come and follow Him. And He gave us, His followers, these instructions: "Go therefore and make disciples of all nations, baptizing them in the name of the Father and of the Son and of the Holy Spirit, teaching them to observe all that I have commanded you" (Matthew 28:19–20 ESV). It is our joy and privilege to join Him in the harvest fields.

He gave his life to free us from every kind of sin,
to cleanse us, and to make us his very own people,
totally committed to doing good deeds.

TITUS 2:14 NLT

PERSONAL APPLICATION:

Where are you patiently sowing seeds of faith? You may not see any fruit right now—or even a bud on a branch—but that does not mean God isn't doing a work under the surface. Don't lose heart. And don't grow weary of doing good. Continue the work God has given you to do; "at the proper time," you *will* "reap a harvest" if you don't give up (Galatians 6:9 NIV).

Who has been a spiritual mother or father to you? Who has invested in your spiritual growth, prayed for you, talked with you, answered your questions, and been there for you? Marmee's family surrounded her with love, gifts, music, and laughter on her birthday—and they took the opportunity to thank her for all she had done for them. May this final picnic scene inspire you to say thank you to one of your spiritual mentors this week. Encourage that person with stories of the harvest that has grown up in your life as a result of their love and faithfulness.

———◦✦◦———

PRAYER FOR TODAY:

Dearest Jesus, thank You for loving me and for giving Your life for me. I praise Your name for all You have done in my life. Help me to give my all to You and invest my whole life into serving You alone. Fill my heart to overflowing with Your love for people. Make me into a fisher of men, women, and children. Show me how I can sow seeds of faith into these people's lives: [specific names]. In Jesus' name, amen.

*Let us not become weary in doing good,
for at the proper time we will reap
a harvest if we do not give up.*

GALATIANS 6:9 NIV

FATHER'S LETTER

WHILE WE WAIT

—◦•◦—

*"And if I go and prepare a place for you,
I will come again and will take you to myself,
that where I am you may be also."*
JOHN 14:3 ESV

> ## "While we wait we may all work, so that these hard days need not be wasted."
>
> [CHAPTER 1]

When he is away during the war, Mr. March writes a letter to his daughters that overflows with "fatherly love and longing for the little girls at home." As you reflect on all that God has been teaching you while reading this book, take a few moments to reread Mr. March's letter. May it be a warm reminder of your heavenly Father's deep love for you:

> *Give them all of my dear love and a kiss. Tell them I think of them by day, pray for them by night, and find my best comfort in their affection at all times. A year seems very long to wait before I see them, but remind them that while we wait we may all work, so that these hard days need not be wasted. I know they will remember all I said to them, that they will be loving children to you, will do their duty faithfully, fight their bosom enemies bravely, and conquer themselves so beautifully that when I come back to them I may be fonder and prouder than ever of my little women.*

Just like the March sisters, we each have seasons of waiting and trials, pain and loss. We endure periods of separation from our loved ones and times of uncertainty. And though it may seem like a long time until you get to see Jesus face-to-face, remember that He has work for you to do *while* you wait. Each day is a gift, full of promise and purpose. No "hard day" is wasted as you watch and wait for Him, share your faith with others, and love people well.

As you continue your pilgrimage here on earth, ask the Holy Spirit to help you do your "duty faithfully," fight your "bosom enemies bravely," and "conquer" yourself beautifully. Continue to open your "guidebook" each day and read it carefully until its pages are well worn. In it you'll find God's encouragement, instructions, and plans for your life. Listen for Jesus to speak. Write down what you hear. And continue to press in.

Finally, keep your eyes turned upward, looking forward to the day when you will be united with Jesus. Imagine the unspeakable joy you'll feel when you see Him. For on that day, He will look at you with eyes of love, fonder and prouder of you than you ever thought possible, and say, "Well done, good and faithful servant" (Matthew 25:23 NIV).

"Seek first the kingdom of God and his righteousness, and all these things will be added to you."

MATTHEW 6:33 ESV

PERSONAL APPLICATION:

A lot of life is spent waiting, but what you do *while you wait* matters. If you're in a waiting time, stay faithful to what God has already told you to do: Love God with *all* that you are and all that you have. Stay consistent with Bible study, prayer, and fellowship. And continue to seek God's kingdom and righteousness first (Matthew 6:33). As you wait patiently for the Lord, He will direct your paths and provide for all your needs.

What are you waiting on God to do? Be encouraged and don't give up. Be like the persistent widow in Luke 18:1–8. Jesus told her story because He wanted to teach us *always* to pray and *never* give up (Luke 18:1). Whatever it is you're waiting for, keep asking, keep seeking, keep knocking (Matthew 7:7 NLT). At just the right time, God will open the right door.

PRAYER FOR TODAY:

Thank You, Jesus, for this reminder to keep working while I wait. Thank You that You're always with me and guiding me. Help me make the most of every day, do my duty faithfully, and serve You well. As I wait for You to speak and move in this area of my life, please grow my reliance on You: [your prayer]. In Jesus' name, amen.

You make known to me the path of life;
in your presence there is fullness of joy;
at your right hand are pleasures forevermore.
PSALM 16:11 ESV

AN INVITATION

*This is real love—not that we loved God, but that he loved us
and sent his Son as a sacrifice to take away our sins.*

1 JOHN 4:10 NLT

No matter where you have been or what your earthly family is like, you have been given a miraculous invitation to become a child of God. Not a day or a moment of your life is wasted or beyond redemption. God loves you with unfailing love and sent His Son, Jesus, to die so that you might be forgiven of your sins and have everlasting life with Him.

Salvation is God's gift to you. All you have to do is trust in Jesus as your Lord and Savior: "If you declare with your mouth, 'Jesus is Lord,' and believe in your heart that God raised him from the dead, you will be saved" (Romans 10:9 NIV). If you want to commit your life to Jesus as your personal Lord and Savior, you can do so by praying a simple prayer from the heart like this:

PRAYER FOR TODAY:

*Dear Jesus, I confess I am a sinner. Please wash me
clean from all my sins and come into my life and heart
forever. I ask You to be my Lord and Savior. I want to be
part of God's family and know You more. Please help me
to grow in my faith and learn to read my Bible and pray.
Thank you for saving me. In Jesus' name, amen.*

NEXT STEPS:

If you prayed that prayer, all of heaven is rejoicing (Luke 15:7)! You are now a child of God and a coheir with Christ. You belong to Jesus forever! Please share this great news with someone special. Make sure you find a church where you can study the Bible and grow in your relationship with God alongside other believers. Your new life with Jesus starts today!

*But to all who did receive him, who believed in his name,
he gave the right to become children of God.*

JOHN 1:12 ESV

AUTHOR'S NOTE

Thank you for taking this pilgrimage with me through the pages of *Little Women*. I pray that this devotional journey has helped you draw closer to the heart of Jesus as you explored His incredible plans and purposes for your life. I hope it has given you a greater sense of your unique place in the body of Christ and inspired you to pursue rich fellowship with other believers.

As I wrote this book, I prayed that Jesus would personalize these messages just for you. That each touching scene from *Little Women* would inspire your faith in a new way. That the verses and prayers would nourish your soul and fill you with hope. And that you might know—more than ever—how wide and long and high and deep is the love of Christ for you (Ephesians 3:18).

I hope you'll share this devotional with others who might need encouragement in their faith. You can also gather around the table with your family members, friends, or sisters in Christ and read it together. (Just don't forget the tissues!) May it be a bridge between a beloved classic novel and "that beautiful old story of the best life ever lived."

If you prayed to receive Jesus as your Savior, made the decision to recommit your life to Christ, or have questions about what it means to be a Christian, I'd love to connect with you! You can find me online at RachelDodge.com to read my blog, send me a message, or link to my social media accounts.

May the Lord bless you and keep you always!

MOMENTS WITH MARMEE

WORDS OF WISDOM FROM MRS. MARCH

Mrs. March is known for her wise counsel and sound advice throughout *Little Women*. Her daughters always know they can come to her for godly insights into their questions and problems. The following are some of her best quotes with chapter references. Enjoy!

"Our burdens are here, our road is before us, and the longing for goodness and happiness is the guide that leads us through many troubles and mistakes to the peace which is a true Celestial City." (ch. 1)

"Now, my little pilgrims, suppose you begin again, not in play, but in earnest, and see how far on you can get before Father comes home." (ch. 1)

"When you feel discontented, think over your blessings, and be grateful." (ch. 4)

"Children should be children as long as they can." (ch. 5)

"Love casts out fear, and gratitude can conquer pride." (ch. 6)

"There is not much danger that real talent or goodness will be overlooked long." (ch. 7)

"My dear, don't let the sun go down upon your anger. Forgive each other, help each other, and begin again tomorrow." (ch. 8)

"It is my greatest happiness and pride to feel that my girls confide in me and know how much I love them." (ch. 8)

"If I don't seem to need help, it is because I have a better friend, even than Father, to comfort and sustain me." (ch. 8)

"My child, the troubles and temptations of your life are beginning and may be many, but you can overcome and outlive them all if you learn to feel the strength and tenderness of your Heavenly Father as you do that of your earthly one. The more you love and trust Him, the nearer you will feel to Him, and the less you will depend on human power and wisdom. His love and care never tire or change, can never be taken from you, but may become the source of lifelong peace, happiness, and strength. Believe this heartily, and go to God with all your little cares, and hopes, and sins, and sorrows, as freely and confidingly as you come to your mother." (ch. 8)

"Money is a needful and precious thing, and when well used, a noble thing, but I never want you to think it is the first or only prize to strive for." (ch. 9)

"Don't you feel that it is pleasanter to help one another, to have daily duties which make leisure sweet when it comes, and to bear and forbear, that home may be comfortable and lovely to us all?" (ch. 11)

"Let me advise you to take up your little burdens again, for though they seem heavy sometimes, they are good for us, and lighten as we learn to carry them." (ch. 11)

"Work is wholesome, and there is plenty for everyone. It keeps us from ennui and mischief, is good for health and spirits, and gives us a sense of power and independence better than money or fashion." (ch. 11)

"Have regular hours for work and play, make each day both useful and pleasant, and prove that you understand the worth of time by employing it well." (ch. 11)

"Go on with your work as usual, for work is a blessed solace. Hope and keep busy, and whatever happens, remember that you never can be fatherless." (ch. 17)

"It is an excellent plan to have some place where we can go to be quiet, when things vex or grieve us." (ch. 20)

"Money is a good and useful thing. . .and I hope my girls will never feel the need of it too bitterly, nor be tempted by too much." (ch. 20)

"In most families there comes, now and then, a year full of events." (ch. 23)

"A kiss for a blow is always best, though it's not very easy to give it sometimes." (ch. 30)

"Mothers may differ in their management, but the hope is the same in all—the desire to see their children happy." (ch. 32)

"Each do our part alone in many things, but at home we work together, always." (ch. 38)

"Go out more, keep cheerful as well as busy, for you are the sunshine-maker of the family, and if you get dismal there is no fair weather." (ch. 38)

"Don't shut yourself up in a bandbox because you are a woman, but understand what is going on, and educate yourself to take your part in the world's work, for it all affects you and yours." (ch. 38)

"Love covers a multitude of sins." (ch. 38)

"Write something for us, and never mind the rest of the world." (ch. 42)

"You have had the bitter, now comes the sweet." (ch. 42)

"Mothers have need of sharp eyes and discreet tongues when they have girls to manage." (ch. 42)

"Don't despond, but hope and keep happy." (ch. 47)

ACKNOWLEDGMENTS

I thank God for every word that's in this book. Every day Jesus met me at the computer, in my Bible readings, on my prayer walks, and in my journal time. All that's beautiful within these pages is because of Him.

I also extend my deepest thanks to the following people who have prayed for me and encouraged me on this journey:

Janet Grant of Books & Such Literary Management for representing me and guiding me in all my bookish endeavors. I couldn't do this without your wisdom and support.

Everyone at Barbour Publishing who helped bring this book to life. Thank you to Annie Tipton for giving me the opportunity to write this book and for all you've done to champion it. Thank you to the marketing and editing teams for all their hard work behind the scenes.

Jeane Wynn for all of her help to promote and publicize my books. Your support makes all the difference!

My steadfast friends and prayer warriors: Courtney Boudreau, Nina Ruth Bruno, Leann Crutchfield, Carolyn Frank, Tammy Gurzhiy, Sarah Magee, Sarah Matye, Hennie McIntire, Krissy Miller, Taylre Nelson, Shauna Pilgreen, and Jenice Williams.

My dear friend, Courtney Boudreau, for all of her love and support. Thank you for having my children over to your house on numerous occasions so I could write, for making all of my small triumphs into jubilees, and for the little gifts you always leave on my doorstep.

My parents, George and Ruth, for praying for me and encouraging me in my faith and in my writing. Thank you, Dad, for being a wonderful first reader. Thank you, Mom, for teaching me to love good books and for introducing me to *Little Women*.

My brother, Matthew, for always cheering me on in all my writing endeavors.

My children, Lizzy and Jack, for your prayers, your love, your back rubs, and your merry hearts. You make my days bright and happy.

And my husband, Bobby, for his encouragement, love, and kindness as I wrote and wrote and wrote. Thank you for checking my references, for helping me brainstorm, and for telling me what to keep and what to skip. Thank you most of all for supporting me in this writing life and for always reminding me that it's all about Jesus.

Finally, thank you to Louisa May Alcott for writing *Little Women* and for reminding us to keep faith and family at the center of our lives. The work of your hands is still bearing fruit today—producing an enduring legacy and a bountiful harvest.

BIBLIOGRAPHY

Alcott, Louisa May. *Little Women (1868, 1869)*. Urbana, IL: Project Gutenberg, 1996.

ABOUT THE AUTHOR

Rachel Dodge is a college English instructor and the bestselling author of *The Anne of Green Gables Devotional: A Chapter-by-Chapter Companion for Kindred Spirits* and *Praying with Jane: 31 Days Through the Prayers of Jane Austen*. She is passionate about encouraging people to grow closer to Jesus through prayer, devotional time, and Bible study. Rachel makes her home in California with her husband, two children, and their snuggly little dog. You can visit her online at RachelDodge.com.

DEVOTIONS FOR KINDRED SPIRITS

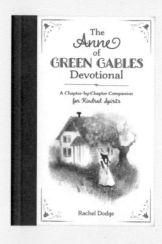

The Anne of Green Gables Devotional offers lovely inspiration that explores the theme of God's love and faithfulness through the pages of the classic L. M. Montgomery novel, cherished by generations of readers. Each reading corresponds with a chapter from the book and invites readers to embrace God's redemptive plans for their lives as His very own adopted daughters in Christ. This beautiful 40-day devotional includes original artwork throughout, and each reading includes examples from the novel, scripture, life application, prayers, and discussion questions perfect for groups, book clubs, or personal reflection.

Hardback / 978-1-64352-616-4 / $16.99